POSSESSING the LAND

5th GRADE

BY CHERIE NOEL

PositiveAction
FOR CHRIST

Possessing The Land

Scripture taken from the *Holy Bible, New International Version,* Copyright © 1973, 1978,
1984 International Bible Society. Used by permission of Zondervan Bible Publishers.

Ninth Printing 2001
Printed in the United States of America
ISBN: 1-929784-20-1

Cover Design by Shannon Brown
Body Design and Artwork by Jesse Snow
Edited by Steve Braswell
Curriculum Consultant: Helen Boen

Published by

Contents

Possessing The Land Scripture Memorization Report Sheet

NAME _____ GRADE _____

TEACHER _____

WEEK	SCRIPTURE	DUE DATE	PARENT'S SIGNATURE
1	Eph. 6:11-12		
2	Eph. 6:13-14		
3	Eph. 6:15-16		
4	Eph. 6:17-18		
5	Eph. 6:19-20		
6	**Eph. 6:11-20**		
7	Matt. 6:19-20		
8	Matt. 6:21-22		
9	Matt. 6:23-24		
10	**Matt. 6:19-24**		
11	Matt. 6:25-26		
12	Matt. 6:27-28		
13	Matt. 6:29-30		
14	Matt. 6:31-32		
15	Matt. 6:33-34		
16	**Matt. 6:25-34**		
17	Psalm 119:1-2		
18	Psalm 119:3-4		
19	Psalm 119:5-6		
20	Psalm 119:7-8		
21	**Psalm 119:1-8**		
22	Psalm 119:9-10		
23	Psalm 119:11-12		
24	Psalm 119:13-14		
25	Psalm 119:15-16		
26	**Psalm 119:9-16**		
27	1 John 4:7-8		
28	1 John 4:9-10		
29	1 John 4:11-12		
30	1 John 4:13-14		
31	**1 John 4:7-14**		
32	1 John 4:15-16		
33	1 John 4:17-19		
34	1 John 4:20-21		
35	**1 John 4:15-21**		

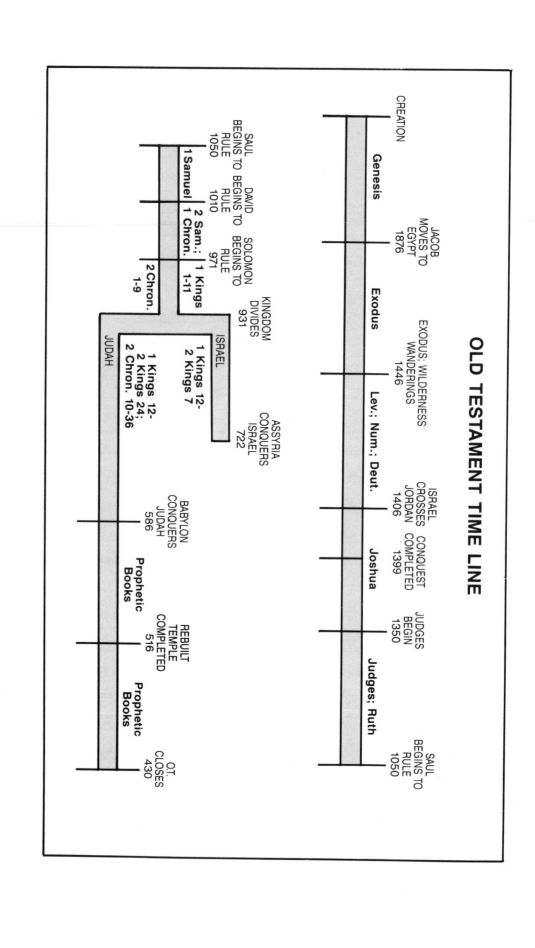

OLD TESTAMENT TIME LINE

1
GOD'S MIRACLE BOOK

Seldom does any book have the name of more than one or two authors. But the Bible was written by forty authors over a period of 1,600 years. The authors were poets, educators, singers, princes, kings, fishermen and statesmen. Some were great scholars while others were unlearned and ignorant men.

Yet each author wrote material which perfectly fits into one book — one story. Why is this true according to 2 Peter 1:21?

_____

_____

_____

VOCABULARY

Doctrine: the principles or teachings of a belief or religion
Rebuke: to criticize or find fault

How long will the Bible last?

Isaiah 40:8 _____

_____

Matthew 24:35 _____

_____

1 Peter 1:23 _____

_____

LIFE PRINCIPLE: The Bible, penned by many authors over a period of many centuries, is a miracle book; for it was truly written by God Himself.

It is more important than any book you will ever own; for after all other books have been destroyed, the Word of God will continue to exist. Never take your Bible for granted, for it is God's Word to man in written form. Your Bible is truly the WORD OF GOD!

Who Teaches Our Hearts?

Since the Bible is God's Word, it needs to be in the center of our lives. Its teachings are more important than anything else we will ever learn. As we read and study the Bible, who is it that teaches our hearts the truths of the Bible? See John 14:26.

_____

_____

_____

Read 1 Corinthians 2:10-13 to learn more about the Holy Spirit. Find the answers to the following questions.

How do we learn the things of God? _____

_____

Where does the Holy Spirit live? _____

_____

Can any man know or understand the things of God without the Holy Spirit? _____

How do we receive the Holy Spirit? See Romans 8:9 and 1 Corinthians 3:16.

_____

_____

_____

The Purposes Of God's Word

Thus the Bible contains precisely the things that God wants us to know, in exactly the form in which He wants us to know them. What was God's primary purpose in giving us the Bible? See John 20:30-31.

_____

_____

Read 2 Timothy 3:15-17. List below some of God's purposes for His Word in your own life.

1. _____

2. _____

3. _____

4. _____

5. _____

6. _____

_____

Look at the words "doctrine" and "rebuke" in the vocabulary list and write their meanings below. Always be sure you understand what God is saying.

Doctrine _____

Rebuke _____

The Beginning And The End

We have learned that the Bible is all one story. The last book of the Bible, which is named _____, is like the close of the story that was begun in the first book of the Bible, which is named _____.

Revelation tells the final story of some of the same things that were first told about in Genesis. Find the final story in the following examples.

Genesis 1:1 says, "In the beginning God created the heavens and the earth." Revelation 21:1 says there will be a _____ _____ .

Genesis 1:5 says, "The darkness he called 'night.' " Revelation 21:25 says, "There will _____."

Genesis 1:16 says, "God made two great lights" (the sun and the moon). Revelation 21:23 says that there will be no need for the _____ or the _____ because the _____ will be our light.

Genesis 2:17 says, "When you eat of it you will surely die." Revelation 21:4 says, "There will be no more _____."

Genesis 3:16 says, "I will greatly increase your pains." Revelation 21:4 says, "There will be no more... _____ _____."

Genesis 3:1-5 says that Satan appears as a deceiver of mankind. Revelation 20:10 describes Satan as "the _____ who _____ them" and says that he will be "thrown into _____ _____."

Genesis 3:24 tells us that Adam and Eve were driven from God's presence because of their sin. Revelation 22:4 says that we shall " _____."

Genesis can be seen, then, as the book of beginnings as it describes the earth God created and man's life on earth as the result of sin. Revelation in the verses you read is describing what it will be like in heaven one day. Thus, from Genesis to Revelation, the Bible is one continuous story. This year, we will be studying the Old Testament to see how God's story unfolds before the birth of Christ. You will learn many important truths for your life as you study.

OLD TESTAMENT

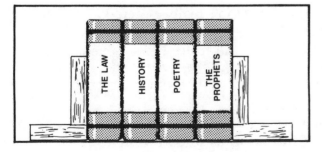

NEW TESTAMENT

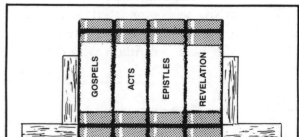

2
SIN AND REDEMPTION

The Bible, God's written Word, is really the story of Jesus Christ. Everything we study in the Bible is there to teach us more about Jesus so that we might become more like Him. We are now beginning our journey through the Old Testament, and there will be many adventures along the way.

Throughout our journey we will learn many great lessons for our lives.

The Book of Genesis presents Jesus as our Creator God. Look up the word "creation" and write its meaning here.

_____

_____

_____

The word "creation" is speaking about beginnings, isn't it? And the Book of Genesis is just that — a book of beginnings. Starting with Genesis 1:1, which says "In the beginning..." Genesis tells the beginning of everything but God! Why doesn't the Bible tell about the beginning of God?

_____

_____

_____

_____

VOCABULARY

Sin: the willful breaking of a religious or moral law
Redemption: to buy back or recover
Civilization: people who have reached a high level of social and cultural development; people who have refined manners
Creation: to bring into being or make out of nothing

The Fall Of Man

The first sin was committed because Adam and Eve didn't really believe God. Find out what happened to Adam and Eve because they didn't believe what God said was true.
■ What did God tell Adam would happen if he ate of the fruit? Read Genesis 2:17.

_____

_____

Notice the word "surely." God means what He said. He knows what is best for us, and He tells us what will result if we disobey. But it is still up to us to do the right thing.

■ When Eve was talking to the serpent (Satan), how did she explain what God had said? Read Genesis 3:3.

_____

_____

_____

■ Satan loves to lie to us. Satan knew God meant what He said, but he still lied to Eve. What did Satan tell Eve in Genesis 3:4?

_____

■ Thus Adam and Eve ate of the fruit and sinned. They had to make a choice. Whose voice did they listen to and believe? _____ What choice did they make? _____

The Results Of Sin

Boys and girls, sin always brings bad results. There were results of sin for Adam and Eve.

LIFE PRINCIPLE: God had warned Adam and Eve of the results of sin, but they chose not to obey. Because of their sin, there have been consequences for all of us.

In the following verses from Genesis 3 and 4, you will see many results of sin that are still part of our lives today.

► Read Genesis 3:6-7. The first thing that Adam and Eve felt was guilt. Adam and Eve had never felt this before because they had never sinned before. But guilt is a feeling that we are very aware of when we disobey God in any way. Our conscience and the Holy Spirit convict us of sin. When God called out to Adam and Eve, they knew they had sinned, and so they felt guilty. They did not have the same relationship with God that they had enjoyed before, and they knew the difference was very great.

► Read Genesis 3:8-10. Adam and Eve's eyes were opened. They realized they were naked, and so they tried to hide themselves from God. When God called out to Adam, he said he hid because he was _____.

► Next God asked Adam why he had eaten the fruit. What was Adam's response?

_____

_____

Next God asked Eve why she had eaten the fruit. What was her response?

_____

_____

Think through Adam and Eve's responses and explain what a third result of sin is.

_____

_____

_____

Thus far we have seen three natural results of sin that appeared in the Garden of Eden when the first sin occurred. These are...

• Guilt
• Fear
• Blaming others

These same three results are evident in our own lives when we sin. Remember to watch for them.

► Read Genesis 3:16-24. List other results of the original sin that are still part of our lives today.

_____

_____

_____

_____

_____

► Another result of sin is seen in the lives of Adam and Eve's children. Read Genesis 4:1-8 and explain what further sins occurred in their family.

_____

_____

_____

_____

_____

_____

Do you think Adam and Eve had seen someone die before? _____

God told Adam and Eve that they would "surely die." By this He meant physical and spiritual death. Can you explain each of these types of death?

Physical death _____

_____

_____

_____

Spiritual death _____

_____

_____

_____

Pictures Of Redemption

The Bible teaches that man's greatest problem is sin, and the root of sin is always lack of faith in God's Word. Copy the last nine words of Romans 14:23 to see the truth of this.

_____

_____

_____

The rest of the Bible shows God's answer to this problem of sin. The answer to the problem is redemption through Jesus Christ. The pages of the Old Testament are filled with TYPES OF CHRIST or pictures of God's plan of redemption through Jesus Christ. Immediately after the original sin, God promised redemption to Adam and Eve. He did this in two ways.

The first promise was in Genesis 3:15. Read this verse and explain the promise.

_____

_____

_____

_____

_____

_____

The second promise was given through something God did in Genesis 3:21. Explain what God did and what this meant.

_____

_____

_____

_____

_____

_____

Names From Genesis 1-5

ACROSS:
2. Satan deceived her.
3. The great deceiver
5. He did not die because God "took him away" (5:24).
7. God was not pleased with his offering of things grown with his own hands.
8. The oldest man who ever lived (5:27)

DOWN:
1. Genesis: The book of _____
3. The son of Adam who continued a spiritual lineage (4:25)
4. He was killed by his brother.
6. He blamed his wife for his sin.

Three Men To Remember

★ A son of Adam who fathered a spiritual lineage was _____ (Genesis 5:3).

★ One of Seth's descendants included a man who did not die. Who was he and what happened to him? (Genesis 5:18 and 24) _____

_____

_____

★ The son of Enoch who is known as the man who lived longest on the earth was

_____

(Genesis 5:21 and 27).

Conquering The Enemy

There were three natural results of sin in the Garden of Eden. Give an example of each of these from your own life.

Guilt _____

_____

_____

Fear _____

_____

_____

Blaming Others _____

_____

_____

3
ABRAHAM AND ISAAC

Another word for "testament" is "covenant." The Old Testament is the covenant God made with man before Jesus Christ came to earth. The word "covenant" means

_____ .

What was the covenant God made with man through Adam and Eve? (Genesis 3:15)

VOCABULARY
Covenant: a binding agreement; a promise

_____

_____

God soon established a race of people that He would use to bring Jesus Christ into the world. This nation was the Hebrew nation or the Jewish nation. Jesus Christ was born of the Jews. God chose a leader for this nation. His name was Abraham. The study of the life of Abraham is of great importance because Abraham was chosen of God to become the father of a new spiritual race.

The Life Of Abraham

Read Genesis 12:1-3, and you will see that God called Abraham for a special task. At the same time, He made a special covenant with Abraham and all those who would become his descendants. List the five promises of God in this important covenant.

1._____

_____

2. _____

_____

3. _____

_____

4. _____

_____

5. _____

_____

This covenant was not only to Abraham but to the Jewish people as well. This was an important promise, for God intended to bring His Son into the world through the descendants of Abraham.

LIFE PRINCIPLE: God always keeps His promises to those who obey His Word.

The life of Abraham was based on obedience to the commands of God and great blessings from God. There were several times when Abraham sinned. Once he lied and said his wife, Sarah, was his sister. Another time, he tried to fulfill God's promise of a son by having a child with his wife's maid. In both these instances, Abraham had severe problems because of his disobedience. But overall, Abraham's life was greatly blessed by God because he trusted God.

Look up the following verses in the Book of Genesis and complete the chart by filling in the following information: (1) the name of the place, (2) the event which occurred there and (3) which character trait(s) were seen in Abraham's life. To help you with the last column, choose from the following list: courage, unselfishness, obedience, reverence and faith.

VERSES	PLACE	EVENT	CHARACTER TRAIT
11:31			None
12:1-5			
12:8			
13:8-9	Bethel		
14:1-2, 12-16			
17:15-16; 20:1; 21:1-3			None
22:1-14			

Abraham's Journeys

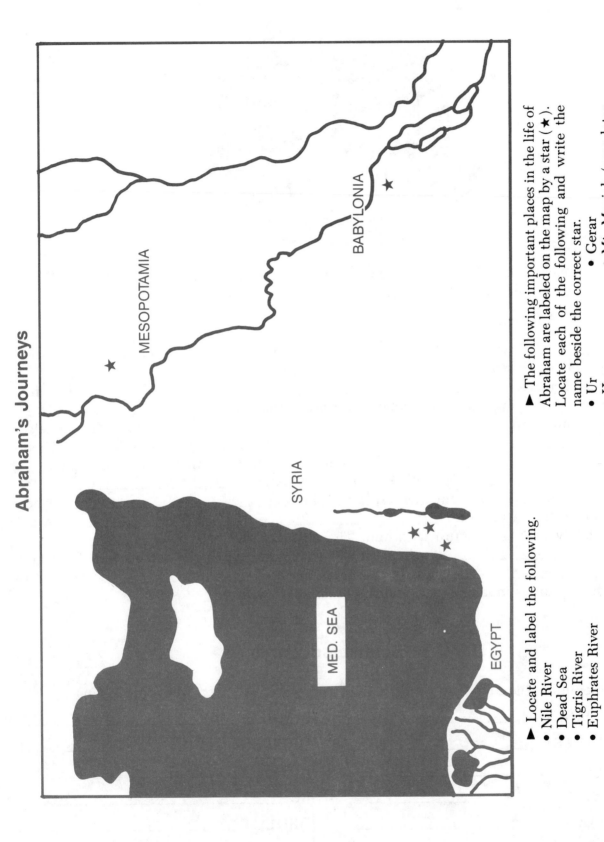

▲ Locate and label the following.
- Nile River
- Dead Sea
- Tigris River
- Euphrates River

▲ The following important places in the life of Abraham are labeled on the map by a star (★). Locate each of the following and write the name beside the correct star.
- Ur
- Haran
- Bethel
- Gerar
- Mt. Moriah (area later known as Jerusalem)

Isaac And Rebekah

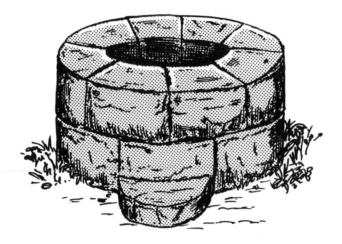

As you read Genesis 24, use the following names to fill in the story of how Abraham used his servant to find a bride for his son.

Abraham   Rebekah   Isaac   servant

_____ wanted his son, _____, to have a wife from his own people. So he sent his trusted _____ to find a wife for _____. In Aram Naharaim the _____ saw _____ for the first time at a spring where she came to fill her water jar. _____ was kind and gave water to the _____ and to his camels. The _____ asked to stay at her father's house. Then _____ went home and told her father what had happened. _____'s brother, Laban, invited the _____ to stay in his home. The servant then explained that _____ had sent him to find a bride for _____. _____ was immediately willing to return with him. The next day, the _____ took _____ and went home. When the camels neared home, _____ was in the field. He saw _____ and brought her to his mother's tent, and she became his wife.

Scrambled Words

Unscramble the following words, names and places all taken from this lesson.

VNCOANET _____   BLEHET _____

MHAARAB _____   HREBAKE _____

SCIAA _____   ARSAH _____

DLBSESE _____   RU _____

NHRAA _____   ORIHAM _____

SRCEDU _____

Conquering The Enemy

When God promised an heir to Abraham and Sarah, it was to be twenty years before the promise was fulfilled. They decided to have a son outside of God's will; and another son, Ishmael, was born of Sarah's handmaid, Hagar. But God still kept His promise, and Isaac was finally born. Later, God tested Abraham's faith by asking him to sacrifice this son. Abraham did not understand God's reasoning at first, but he did not trust his own understanding. He obeyed God because he trusted God.

God will test your faith many times also. Do you trust God enough to obey Him in all things? Think of some ways in which it is difficult for you to obey, but you can see that they might be ways in which God is testing your faith._____

_____

_____
_____
_____

God wants you to learn a lesson from Isaac as well. Isaac was obedient to his father even if it would have meant death. God wants us to love, respect and obey our parents in all things even if we do not understand. If we are obedient to our parents, then God will bless our lives. Read Genesis 26:12-14 and tell how God blessed this obedient and loving son._____

_____
_____
_____

4
JACOB AND ESAU

Isaac and his wife Rebekah had twin sons —Jacob and Esau. Esau was born just before Jacob, and so he was considered to be the firstborn. This held many advantages. Esau was a hunter and loved to be in the woods and fields. Jacob was his mother's favorite and enjoyed staying closer to home. Rebekah wanted Jacob to have the advantages of being the firstborn and helped him deceive Isaac and Esau. The story of Jacob and Esau is a story of deception. As you study this story, think about the good and bad character qualities in Jacob and Esau.

The Birthright

Read the story in Genesis 25:27-34. In your own words, explain how Jacob used craftiness to obtain Esau's birthright._____

_____

_____

_____

_____

VOCABULARY

Sow: to plant for growing; to scatter or spread

Reap: to gather; to obtain as a reward

Birthright: privileges or rights a person has by birth. In Old Testament times, this included material and spiritual possessions as well as the right to be the head of the family. This was given to the firstborn son.

Blessing: the giving of special favor and success

Crafty: sly; cunning; deceitful

Deceit (deception): lying to make someone believe something that is not true; to mislead; a dishonest action

Having the birthright was an important possession. It was the natural inheritance of the firstborn son. Having the birthright meant you had the following advantages:
★ It meant you would one day be the head of your family or tribe.
★ It meant you would receive many material possessions—including twice the property when your father died.
★ It meant you would receive spiritual blessings—receiving the promises given to Abraham and becoming the ancestor of Jesus.

Thus, ownership of the birthright was very important. In what ways do you think both Jacob's and Esau's attitudes in this situation were wrong?

JACOB'S ATTITUDE	ESAU'S ATTITUDE

The Stolen Blessing

But the birthright was not all that Jacob wanted. Years later, Rebekah and Jacob together used deception to take what they wanted. Read chapter 27 of Genesis to understand this part of the story. Match the following sentence beginnings with the correct endings.

_____1. Isaac was old, and...

_____2. Isaac asked Esau to get food for him so he might...

_____3. Rebekah told Jacob to...

_____4. Jacob tricked Isaac by...

_____5. Isaac was deceived because...

_____6. Isaac gave the blessing...

_____7. Esau came back and learned...

_____8. Esau was so upset that he planned...

A. To kill his brother.

B. Take food to Isaac to receive the blessing before Esau returned.

C. He believed Jacob was Esau.

D. That his father had been deceived.

E. His eyes were weak.

F. Give him his blessing before he died.

G. Covering his neck and arms with goatskin.

H. To Jacob.

Sowing And Reaping

The principle of sowing and reaping is stated in Galatians 6:7. Find the verse and write it here. _____

_____

_____

_____

LIFE PRINCIPLE: Whatever a person does, whether it be good or bad, will come back to him as it was done.

In other words, the things you do will come back to you. If you sow obedience, blessings will come back to you. If you hurt others, others will hurt you. If you spread joy to others, joy will come back to you. And if, like Jacob, you sow lies and deception, deception will come back to you.

The first thing that came back to Jacob

and Rebekah because of their sinfulness is found in Genesis 27:41-43. What happened and why?

_____

_____

_____

_____

_____

_____

The second story shows in a more real way the principle of sowing and reaping. When Jacob left home, he went to Haran to live with his Uncle Laban. Remember, Laban was the brother of Rebekah. You first learned of him when Abraham sent his servant to find a wife for Isaac. Read Genesis 29 and answer the following questions.

* * * * * *

• Whom did Jacob want to marry? _____

• For which girl did he work for seven years? _____

• Who deceived him by giving him the older daughter as his wife? _____

• Who became Jacob's first wife? _____

• For whom did Jacob work for another seven years? _____

• Who was Jacob's beloved wife? _____

• Who gave birth to many sons? _____

Many years later, Jacob knew God wanted him to return home. So he took his wives, children, servants and all his animals and returned to his homeland. On his journey home, he had an encounter with God. After wrestling with an angel, God changed Jacob's name to _____ (Genesis 32:28). As he went to meet Esau for the first time after many years, he was concerned about his brother's attitude toward him. Remember he had not seen Esau since he fled after having deceived

him. Describe what the meeting was like according to Genesis 33:1-4. _____

_____

_____

_____

_____

_____

_____

Beginning with the first letter write every third letter to begin the key verse of this lesson. Then complete the verse.

G I J O K R D O S C E X A U L N M E N S T O O D T C F B H O E
E S M A N O M R C B U K H L E A E D E M A N W M C B A O A N

" ___ ___ ___ ___ ___ ___ ___ ___

___ ___ ___ ___ ___ ___ ___ ___. ___

___ ___ ___ _____ "

Conquering The Enemy

• It is very easy to fall into the sin of deception. We all want our own way at times; or we become jealous of what someone else has, and we try to find a way to get what we want. It is important to learn to recognize this sin. Can you think of one or two times when you deceived someone in order to get your way?

Explain. _____

_____

_____

_____

_____

_____

_____

• It is also a sign of maturity to begin to learn the principle of sowing and reaping. We can see this principle at work both when we do right and when we do wrong. On the chart below share several instances from your own life when this principle was at work. Share both good and bad instances.

I SOWED...	I REAPED...
• _____	• _____
_____	_____
_____	_____
• _____	• _____
_____	_____
_____	_____
• _____	• _____
_____	_____
_____	_____

5
THE STORY OF JOSEPH

Because of sin, throughout Jacob's life, there were problems within his family. His wives were jealous of each other. Leah and his wives' handmaids had ten sons. For many years, Rachel was unable to have children. Finally, after many years, she had a son that was named Joseph. Because Joseph was born of his favorite wife, Rachel, he became Jacob's favorite son. This also caused many problems with all of his sons.

Jacob Meets With God

In spite of his family troubles, God kept his promise to Jacob. When Jacob first left his home, God appeared to him in a dream and renewed the promise he had given man

---

VOCABULARY

Exalt: to raise in status; to praise
Humble: modest; showing awareness of one's imperfections

---

years earlier. List the key ideas in the promise found in Genesis 28:12-16. _____

_____

_____

_____

_____

_____

_____

_____

These were the same promises that were given to _____.

Years later, when Jacob returned home, he again had a meeting with God. During the night, Jacob wrestled with an angel of the Lord and asked for a blessing. It was at this time that he was given a new name. Jacob's name was now changed to _____ (Genesis 32:28), which means "he struggles with God." This was the name of the nation which God had first promised to Abraham. Jacob's sons were to be ancestors of the great nation of Israel. Thus Jacob's twelve sons would become the leaders of the twelve tribes of Israel.

The Twelve Sons Of Jacob

Unscramble the following words to find the names of Jacob's (Israel's) twelve sons and thus the names of the tribes of Israel. Use Genesis 29:32-30:24 and 35:18 if you need help with the names. (Note: Levi was later not considered as one of the twelve tribes because they were the priests of Israel. Joseph was not a tribe because his two sons became the heads of two tribes—Ephraim and Manasseh.)

- ADG _____
- IVLE _____
- DHAJU _____
- BEENRU _____
- NAD _____
- BLUUNEZ _____

- SHEOPJ _____
- SCHAARIS _____
- THAAILNP _____
- MANBIJEN _____
- REHAS _____
- MISNOE _____

Joseph's Victories Over Trials

The story of Joseph is of a God-fearing young man who had unusual courage and character. Several times in his life, he was faced with great temptations, but he handled himself wisely. He had the courage to do what was right, and God greatly blessed him.

Number the following parts of Joseph's life in the correct order in which they happened. The chapter references from the Book of Genesis may be of help if you need them.

_____ Joseph was the firstborn son of Rachel (30).
_____ Pharaoh puts Joseph in charge of the whole land of Egypt, second only to Pharaoh himself (41).
_____ Joseph interprets the dreams of Pharaoh's cupbearer and baker (40).
_____ Joseph is the favorite son of Jacob, his father (37).
_____ Potiphar's wife tries to get Joseph to commit adultery. When he refuses, she lies to her husband about Joseph's actions (39).
_____ Joseph interprets Pharaoh's dream telling him to plan for the famine to come (41).
_____ Joseph is hated by his brothers (37).
_____ Joseph is put in charge of the household of Potiphar, an official of Pharaoh (39).
_____ Pharaoh learns of Joseph's divine revelations of dreams and asks him to interpret his dream (41).
_____ Joseph is sold as a slave to traders going to Egypt (37).
_____ Joseph's master sends him to prison where he spends two years (39).
_____ Joseph's family comes to Egypt during the famine; Joseph is reunited with his father and forgives his brothers (42-47).

An important principle at work in Joseph's life is found in Romans 8:28. Copy this verse here. _____

_____

_____

_____

LIFE PRINCIPLE: God does not promise us that we will not be tempted. He does not promise that things will always go well in every circumstance. But God does promise to bless our lives and to work in all things for the good of those who love Him.

Joseph: An Example Of Forgiveness

Copy the words of Joseph as he greets the brothers who had sold him into slavery years before. They are found in Genesis 45:5. _____

_____

_____

What else did he do to help his father and brothers? (Genesis 45) _____

_____

_____

_____

The Sons Of Promise

Complete the following puzzle with the names of some of the "sons of promise."

Abraham's son of promise	_ S _ _ _
The deceiver	_ _ _ O _
Son of a maidservant (30:5-6)	_ _ N
Abraham's firstborn son	_ S _ _ _ _ _
	O
	F
Jacob's favored son	_ _ _ _ P _
Jacob's name changed to	_ _ R _ _ _
A son of Leah (29:33)	_ _ _ _ O _
Rachel died when this son was born	_ _ _ _ _ M _ _
Became a tribe of priests (29:34)	_ _ _ I
Had the birthright first	_ S _ _
Leah's first son (29:32)	_ _ _ _ E _

Conquering The Enemy

Joseph had several instances in which he had to trust God to make something good out of something evil. God definitely did this for Joseph. Tell of an instance in your life in which God took something that seemed bad or wrong and worked it out for your good. _____

_____

_____

_____

_____

_____

Is there something happening right now that you do not understand, but you will trust God to work it out for good? _____ Explain. _____

_____

_____

_____

What then should a Christian do when he/she has troubles or difficulties?

_____

_____

_____

_____

6
THE EFFECTS OF SIN

LIFE PRINCIPLE: We must learn to distinguish between Satan's deceptive voice and God's clear teachings.

In the Book of Genesis we saw clear examples of both Satan's deceptive voice and God's clear teachings. Jacob was often deceived by listening to the wrong voice. Joseph was placed where he was because he listened to and obeyed the voice of God.

Now because of the famine in Israel, Joseph's brothers and many other Hebrews went into the land of Egypt to live. Read Genesis 50:22-23. Joseph saw many generations follow him into the land of Egypt.

Egypt is a picture of sin. Satan uses sin to keep us in bondage or slavery to himself. Satan does not want us free to serve the Lord. Thus, sin is a horrible problem; for every time we sin, we are actually showing that a part of us is in bondage to Satan.

The Israelites In Egypt

► Read Exodus 1:7 to see the effects of sin. The Israelites had gone into Egypt for food. But what happened to them while they were in Egypt? _____

_____

_____

_____

► Read Exodus 1:8-9. Joseph, an Israelite, had been in charge of Egypt. But many years had passed, and Joseph was dead. The new king did not know Joseph. How did this king feel about the Israelites? _____

_____

_____

_____

VOCABULARY

Temptation: to be attracted or enticed to do something immoral or wrong
Bondage: slavery; subject to an outside force
Slave master: someone who assigns work or places a burden on someone else, usually in a severe manner
Oppress: to control or rule by cruel or unjust means
Ruthlessly: without pity or mercy
Mortar: a mixture used between bricks or stones to hold them together

► Read Exodus 1:10. What did the king think might happen if they didn't put controls over the Israelites? _____

_____

_____

_____

► Read Exodus 1:11-14. Describe the life of the Israelites in Egypt. Make sure you look up and know the following words and use them correctly in your description: slave masters, oppress, dread, ruthlessly, forced labor, bondage, mortar.

_____

_____

_____

_____

_____

_____

The Power Of Satan

We can easily see the hand of Satan working in this time of bondage. We need to understand how Satan works so we can learn to resist him, for the Bible says in James 4:7 that if we resist the Devil,

_____ .

To find out who the Devil is, read Isaiah 14:12-15 and answer the following questions.

■ Where did the Devil first live? _____

■ What was his name before he fell? _____

■ Satan used one phrase five different times. What was this phrase? _____
What sin does this show? _____

■ Why did God have to make Lucifer leave heaven? _____

_____

Now, to find out even more about this enemy, look up the following Scriptures.

■ 2 Corinthians 4:4. What kind of god is the Devil? _____

_____

■ Ephesians 2:2. Over what power is the Devil the ruler? _____

_____

■ Hebrews 2:14. What other power does the Devil possess? _____

_____

■ 1 Peter 5:8. Does the Devil ever have your best interests in mind? _____

How To Resist Temptation

Read Luke 4:1-13. Christ Himself was tempted by Satan. Many people do not want to believe that the Devil really exists, but Christ knew very well of his existence.

In this story, Satan tempted Christ three times, and each time He resisted the Devil's temptation. Find the answers Christ gave to Satan.

VERSES	HOW SATAN TEMPTED CHRIST	WORDS THAT DEFEATED SATAN
Luke 4:1-4		
Luke 4:5-8		
Luke 4:9-12		

Jesus Christ had a good deal more to say about Satan. Read the following verses and write what Christ said about Satan in each.

• Matthew 13:38 _____

• John 8:44 _____

• John 12:31 _____

Christ knew how to defeat Satan. He used the Word of God. This is the reason why you should know the Word of God thoroughly—you need God's Word to defeat Satan.

Puzzle

Use the following words to complete the puzzle.

BIRTHRIGHT   DECEIVE   TEMPTATION   COVENANT
DECEPTION   OPPRESS   CRAFTINESS   SIN
REDEMPTION   SLAVE MASTER   CREATION   BONDAGE

ACROSS:
5. Using lies and being misleading
6. Lying to make someone believe something that is not true
7. Someone who places a burden of work on others (2 words)
8. To control or rule by cruel or unjust means
10. Slavery
12. Privileges given to the firstborn son

DOWN:
1. To buy back
2. An enticement to do something wrong
3. A binding agreement or promise
4. Bring into being out of nothing
9. Slyness; deceitfulness
11. Iniquity

Unscramble the circled letters to see who can always defeat Satan. ___ ___ ___ ___ ___

Conquering The Enemy

Is it a sin to be tempted? _____

When does temptation become sin?

_____

_____

In Luke 4:13, the Devil is said to have departed "until an opportune time." What does this mean?

_____

_____

How does this apply to you? _____

_____

_____

7
THE HEBREW NATION IN BONDAGE

The Israelites were the people chosen by God to bring the Savior into the world. They are often called the Jews. Jesus Christ was born a Jew. The Jews are thus very important to God as well as to us.

Today our world is full of unrest, trouble, wars, thefts and murders. Many people are worried; they wonder if God knows what is going on. The Israelites, in Egypt, also wondered if God knew what was happening to them. It seemed to them that God had forgotten them, for He had allowed them to be in terrible slavery for over 400 years. Do you not imagine that they felt God no longer cared? Everyone can have that feeling when things are not going well.

When problems and tribulations do happen, we have to remember and trust in Romans 8:28. As a review, explain the promise of that verse. _____

_____

_____

_____

According to this verse, to whom is this promise made? _____

_____

Notice the words "His purpose." The entire Book of Exodus teaches us that God has a purpose and plan for all He does. Man may fail, and Satan may attack; yet God has His plan. There can be joy and peace in the thought that we are in God's plan and under His protection. Copy Romans 8:31 and see how God states this idea.

_____

_____

_____

_____

VOCABULARY

Pharaoh: the title of a ruler in ancient Egypt
Foreknew: to have known personally beforehand
Predestined: foreordained by divine decree
Justified: to be declared free from blame or guilt
Glorified: to be made like Jesus Christ in heaven
"Conformed to the likeness of his Son": to become like Jesus Christ in our actions and attitudes.

God Fulfills His Plan

God had a plan for the Jewish nation. He wanted them to become a strong and united nation. He wanted them to develop strength of character to withstand hardship. He also wanted them to desire to return to the Promised Land—the land He had first promised to Abraham.

God has plans for all who belong to Him.

Read Romans 8:28 again and then study verses 29 and 30. There are four words in these verses that help to explain His overall plan. Write the words and then their meanings. The first letter of each word is given to help you.

* * * * * *

■ F _____

_____

■ P _____

_____

■ J _____

_____

■ G _____

_____

God Calls A Leader

To work out His purpose, God always uses people. God had chosen Moses to be the leader of the Jewish nation. Moses was chosen for this job even before he was born just as God has a plan for your life already in mind.

But when Moses was born, there were already problems to be worked out in his life. Satan was trying to destroy God's plan, for the Pharaoh had given the following command. See Exodus 1:22. _____

_____

_____

_____

Moses' mother was a very godly woman who trusted God to take care of this great tribulation. Thus, when Moses was born, God led her to hide her baby in a basket in the river. His sister, Miriam, watched over her baby brother. It is fun to see how God works out His plan. Read what God did in Exodus 2:5-10 to protect the child whom He had chosen.

★ Who saw the boat among the reeds and sent a slave girl to get it? _____

_____

★ Who volunteered to get a nurse for the baby? _____
★ Whom did she get to be the baby's nurse? _____

Thus, for several years the baby stayed in his own home. There his parents faithfully taught him about the Lord. Then the day came when Moses went to live at the palace. There the Egyptian princess called him her son. What do you think God's purpose was for this part of Moses' life?

_____

_____

_____

_____

_____

In the palace, the young prince had everything he could want. He lived in the luxurious palace and attended fine schools. Egyptian students learned to read and write. They studied science, astronomy, mathematics and music. But Moses never forgot that he was an Israelite. His relatives were slaves.

In God's timing, this part of Moses' life came to an abrupt end. The story is found in Exodus 2:11-15. Fill in the blanks to explain this important event.

* * * * * *

Moses was walking among the Hebrew slaves and watched them at their _____ _____. When he saw one of the slaves being beaten, he _____ the Egyptian and _____ his body. The next day, Moses saw two _____ fighting. One asked if Moses was thinking of _____ him as he had killed the _____. Moses was afraid the act that he had done in secret had become known. When _____ heard of this, he tried to _____ Moses. Moses fled from Pharaoh and went to live in _____.

Thus began the second portion of Moses' life. Moses' life can be divided into three periods of forty years each:
• Forty years in Egypt as the son of Pharaoh's daughter
• Forty years in the desert of Midian
• Forty years as the leader of Israel

Conformed To Christ's Likeness

Forty years is a long time to wait, isn't it? And yet God had Moses wait for two periods of forty years before He was ready to use him. In the verses in Romans that we have been studying, God uses the phrase "conformed to the likeness of his Son." What do you think this means? _____

_____

_____

_____

_____

What then do you think God's purpose was for Moses during the forty years he spent in the wilderness? _____

_____

_____

_____

_____

Sometimes we get anxious to know God's plans right now.

LIFE PRINCIPLE: We must always remember that God's primary purpose is to develop the inner character of His Son Jesus Christ in us.

Psalm 27:14 and 32:8 both tell us to trust God in this way. Explain in your own words what these verses mean. _____

_____

_____

_____

The Character Of Moses

Moses had true *inner character*. But what are some of the things that make for good inner character? To find out, read the verses listed below and look for the right word to complete the spaces beside each verse.

Colossians 1:9	_ I _ _ _ _
Titus 3:2	_ _ N _ _ _ _ _ _ _
2 Peter 1:5	_ N _ _ _ _ _ _ _
2 Corinthians 10:5	_ _ E _ _ _ _ _
Hebrews 12:28	_ _ _ _ R _ _ _ _
Colossians 3:12	_ _ _ _ _ _ C _
Psalm 31:24	H _ _ _
1 Peter 3:8	_ _ _ _ A _ _ _ _ _ _ _
Ephesians 4:32	_ _ R _ _ _ _ _ _
James 1:4	_ _ _ _ _ _ _ A _ _
2 Peter 1:6	_ _ _ _ - C _ _ _ _ _
Colossians 3:12	_ _ _ T _ _ _ _ _ _
1 Timothy 4:8	_ _ _ _ _ _ E _ _
Psalm 34:17	R _ _ _ _ _ _ _ _

Conquering The Enemy

God has a purpose for your life also. As we have learned, His main purpose is to conform you so that your inner character will become more like that of Jesus Christ. What are some of the things God is using in your life right now to accomplish this? Some of these are listed below. Beside each write a specific example of what God is doing in that area of your life to accomplish His plan.

• People— _____

_____

_____

_____

• Places— _____

_____

_____

• Situations— _____

_____

_____

• Problems— _____

_____

_____

• Friends— _____

_____

_____

EXODUS

8 THE PLAGUES AND THE PASSOVER

Plagues Upon Egypt

VOCABULARY

Passover: a Jewish celebration commemorating the deliverance of the Hebrews from slavery in Egypt

Plague: an affliction or torment

Gnats: small insect-type parasites on men and animals

Defect: fault or blemish

Locust: a large insect related to the grasshopper

Hyssop: a fragrant plant of the mint family

Yeast: any substance which causes dough to rise

The Egyptians and their ruler, Pharaoh, trusted in false gods. They worshiped the Nile River, the sun and even flies and frogs. They honored the ox and the cow. God wanted to show that He was the one true God—the all-powerful One. God would show His power over the same things that Pharaoh worshiped.

God had promised the Israelites their freedom, but of course Pharaoh was not willing to let God's people leave Egypt. God caused ten plagues or signs to happen in Egypt to show His power and to make Pharaoh willing to let the people go. And it was Moses whom God used to accomplish this task.

All verses used in the following charts are from the Book of Exodus. Look up each passage and then fill in the rest of the chart.

EXODUS	DESCRIPTION OF THE PLAGUE	THE RESPONSE
7:19-25		Could the magicians do this? _____ Pharaoh's heart became _____. As with many of the other plagues, this one had to do with something the Egyptians worshiped—the Nile River.

EXODUS	DESCRIPTION OF THE PLAGUE	THE RESPONSE
8:1-15		Could the magicians do this? ____ What did Pharaoh promise? _____ _____ Pharaoh _____ his _____.
8:16-19		Could the magicians do this? ____ What did the magicians say to Pharaoh? _____ _____ Pharaoh's heart was _____ .
8:20-32		What did Pharaoh promise? _____ _____ Did he keep his promise? _____
9:1-7		Did this plague happen to Egyptians and Hebrews? _____ What was the difference? _____ _____ _____ Pharaoh's heart was _____.
9:8-12		How do you know the magicians had no control over this plague? _____ _____ The Lord _____ Pharaoh's heart.
9:22-35		What did Pharaoh admit? (9:27) _____ _____ What did Pharaoh promise? (9:28) _____ Did he keep his promise? (9:34-35) _____ Pharaoh's heart was _____.

EXODUS	DESCRIPTION OF THE PLAGUE	THE RESPONSE
10:12-20		What did Pharaoh admit again? _____ _____ _____ Did Pharaoh let the Hebrews go this time? _____
10:21-27		What was it like in the Jewish homes? _____ What did Pharaoh tell Moses? (10:28) _____ _____ The Lord _____ Pharaoh's heart.

The Purposes Of The Plagues

How many plagues have been brought on Egypt now? _____ The Egyptians had many superstitious ideas. They had magicians who could perform many feats. When the first plagues occurred, Pharaoh probably thought they were done by Hebrew magicians. His own magicians were able to do the first two plagues. This is because they were given power by _____. But only God can give life or take life away. So when gnats were formed from dust, the magicians could not duplicate this feat. When the boils broke out, the magicians were also covered.

God had three purposes for the plagues He brought upon the people. Find the reasons in these verses and write them out.

* * * * * *

■ Genesis 15:13-14— _____

_____

■ Exodus 9:13— _____

_____

■ Exodus 9:16— _____

_____

Pharaoh was a powerful ruler. But God is all-powerful. The efforts of an Egyptian ruler to defy the Almighty came to nothing.

LIFE PRINCIPLE: God's power truly controls the universe.

The Passover

Now Moses told Pharaoh the tenth plague would fall—the severest of all! Fill in the blanks after reading Exodus 12:1-33.

God told each household of the Israelites to kill a _____ without _____. Its blood was to be put on the _____ and _____ of the doorframe with a "bunch of _____." The lamb had to be _____ with herbs and bread made without _____. Anything that was left over had to be _____. At _____ the Lord struck down all the _____ in Egypt including that of the livestock. However, those homes which had _____ over the doorframes were passed over. Then Pharaoh ordered the Israelites to _____ Egypt. The Egyptians wanted them to hurry before they were all _____.

This important night is still celebrated each year by Jews all over the world. It is called the Passover. This celebration is to celebrate the fact that the Lord delivered them from bondage. Explain what the word "Passover" means. _____

_____

_____

_____

_____

_____

The Israelites were finally allowed to leave Egypt and return to the Promised Land as God desired them to do. Four hundred years before, only seventy had come with Jacob (Israel) to find Joseph in Egypt. Now there were almost three million Israelites going back to Canaan.

Within a few days, Pharaoh felt sorry he had allowed the Israelites to leave Egypt. He then took an army of men on chariots and horses. The Israelites crossed the Red Sea when God made the sea open up to dry land. As Pharaoh followed on the dry land into the sea, the sea rolled back and drowned him and all his men. The Israelites were safe.

Israel's Deliverance From Egypt

Locate and write in the following places on the map.

- Egypt
- Canaan
- Sinai Peninsula
- Jerusalem
- Mediterranean Sea
- Dead Sea
- Jordan River
- Red Sea

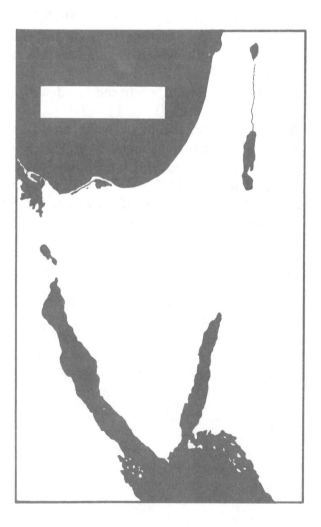

Puzzle

1. _____ _____ _____ | | _____
2. _____ _____ _____ | | _____
3. _____ | | _____ _____ _____ _____ _____
4. _____ _____ _____ | |
5. _____ | | _____ _____ _____
6. _____ | | _____ _____
7. _____ _____ _____ | | _____
8. _____ _____ _____ | | _____ _____
9. _____ _____ _____ | | _____
10. _____ _____ _____ _____ _____ _____ _____

11.

1. Not life, but _____ (Deut. 30:15)
2. "Dead _____ give perfume a bad smell" (Eccl. 10:1).
3. Lev. 11 tells which _____ are clean (they may be eaten) and which are unclean (11:46-47).
4. Farmers should honor the Lord with the firstfruits of their _____ (Prov. 3:9).
5. A life sustainer (Lev. 17:11)
6. "_____ and fire mixed with blood...was hurled down upon the earth" (Rev. 8:7).
7. "Evil spirits that looked like _____" (Rev. 16:13)
8. John ate _____ and wild honey (Mark 1:6).
9. God wanted to show His _____ through Pharaoh (Ex. 9:16).
10. "Total _____ covered all Egypt for three days" (Ex. 10:22).
11. The _____ _____ (Ex. 7-12)

9
GOD GIVES THE LAW

God's people, the Israelites, had lived in Egypt, a heathen land, for over 400 years. During that time, they had no word from God. There was no temple in which they could worship and learn of God's plan for them. They did not know everything of what God expected of them or how He wanted them to live. Instead, they had learned about the ways and laws of the Egyptians.

Of course, many of the Israelites, such as Moses' family and Joshua's family, believed in God and trusted Him to one day deliver them. But many other Israelites no longer believed. This was one reason, remember, that God had for the plagues, to help them believe once again.

But now God saw that the people needed a set of laws so they would know how to live together. The people had been traveling for several months and were ready to hear God's laws. Moses went up to Mt. Sinai for three days. After that time, thunder and lightning came from the mountain, and the Israelites heard God's laws.

The Ten Commandments

Read the Ten Commandments in Exodus 20:1-17 and complete the commandments below. Then match the commandment from the left column with statements in the right column to make sure you understand their meanings.

1. "You shall have no other _____ before me."
2. "You shall not make for yourself an _____ in the form of anything in _____
or on the _____
or in the _____.
You shall not _____ down to them or _____ them."
3. "You shall not misuse the _____ of the Lord your God."

_____ Never tell a lie.

_____ Husbands and wives should be true to each other.

_____ Never use God's name in swearing or in foolish talk.

_____ Do not kill.

4. "Remember the _____ day by keeping it _____."

5. "Honor your _____ and your _____."

6. "You shall not _____."

7. "You shall not commit _____."

8. "You shall not _____."

9. "You shall not give _____ _____ against your neighbor."

10. "You shall not _____...anything that belongs to your _____."

_____ Never greedily wish for something that belongs to someone else.

_____ Respect your parents.

_____ Never cheat or steal.

_____ Worship only the true God.

_____ Keep God's special day.

_____ Never worship or pray to a picture or an image.

The Law: God's Mirror

In the Ten Commandments, God is showing how holy He really is because God demands perfection. The Ten Commandments are the law of God. To see this, copy James 2:10 and then explain the verse here. _____

_____

_____

_____

Can you keep all of God's law? _____ The law demands and expects a perfect life to satisfy God. But, we know that none of us can live a perfect life especially when we understand how perfect God is. Why was the law given to us then if no one can keep it? See Romans 3:20 to help you with your answer. _____

_____

_____

_____

_____

> LIFE PRINCIPLE: The law is God's mirror to show us how sinful we are.

The law cannot cleanse us from sin, but it does show us our problem. A mirror will show us that our face is soiled, but the mirror cannot wash us clean.

The Golden Calf

By this time, the Hebrews had witnessed many miracles of God. They had seen the ten plagues. They had witnessed the events of the Passover. They had been given a great leader.

They had seen the parting of the Red Sea for their deliverance. They had seen Pharaoh's army drown in that same sea. They had been led by God into the desert and fed and cared for by Him.

It would seem that they would have great faith in God by this time; but as soon as Moses had gone up Mt. Sinai to receive God's law, the people reverted to their old ways once again. Read Exodus 32:1-4 and explain what the people did. _____

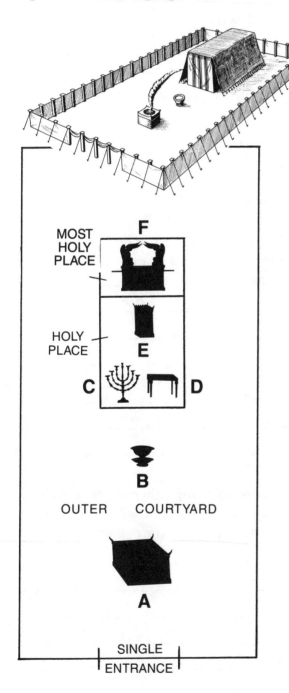

_____

_____

_____

_____

Which of the commandments had been broken by their actions? _____

_____

_____

_____

The Tabernacle

THE TABERNACLE: A sacred tent and its furniture made according to a plan given by God to Moses on the mount. Its purpose was to meet the needs of the nation for sacrifice and worship.

Once God had judged the Israelites for their sin of false worship (of their golden calf), it was time to instruct the people in true worship. Part of the instructions God gave Moses while he was on the mount included the plan for the tabernacle. The tabernacle itself was inside a large tent with a large outer courtyard. There was only one entrance to the courtyard. Upon first entering the courtyard, you would immediately approach the Bronze Altar (A). The purpose of this was for burnt offerings and sacrifices. Further in was the Bronze Basin (B), which was used by the priests to wash themselves and the sacrifices.

The tabernacle itself was divided into two parts—the Holy Place and the Most Holy Place. The Holy Place contained the Golden Lampstand (C), the Golden Table (D) and the Altar of Incense (E).

The Most Holy Place contained the Ark of the Covenant (F), a sacred chest which was a symbol of the divine presence. A curtain of costly material separated the two sections. No one except the high priest ever entered the Most Holy Place; and he went in only once a year, on the Day of Atonement, to make atonement for the sins of the people.

Every detail of the tabernacle was a type of Jesus Christ. To better see this, place the letter of the piece of furniture which seems to describe one of the following pictures of Christ.

_____ He is our sin sacrifice.
_____ He is the light of the world.
_____ We pray in His name.

_____ God's dwelling place is holy.
_____ He is the bread of life.
_____ He cleanses us from sin.

Why do you think God only provided one entrance to the tabernacle? _____
_____
_____

Conquering The Enemy

Can you obey all the law of God? _____ Who was able to obey all the law? _____ Does obeying the law take away our sin? _____ Since the law shows us our sin, how can we be cleansed? _____
_____
_____
_____

Let's relate some of the commandments to problems we face in today's world.
• What types of things could become "gods" in your life? _____
_____
_____

• Do you ever hear others misusing the name of the Lord or using other types of bad or crude language? _____ Have you ever been tempted to do so also? _____
• In what ways are you tempted to dishonor or show disrespect to your parents? _____
_____
_____
_____

• How is hatred like murder? _____
Do you ever feel hatred or jealousy toward others? _____

When? _____

_____

_____

• In what ways are you tempted to lie, cheat or steal? _____

_____

_____

When we disobey in any of the above areas, we are breaking one of the Ten Commandments. This shows us again that we cannot keep ourselves perfect and that we need Jesus Christ to be our Savior. When we do sin, what should be our response? _____

_____

_____

_____

10
THE WAY TO GOD

One of Jacob's (Israel's) sons was named Levi. Levi became the head of the tribe called the Levites. The Levites became the priestly tribe, and Leviticus is named after them. It is a book for priests and for the people on how to worship God.

The Theme Of Leviticus

The main theme of the Book of Leviticus is "holiness." Look up the word "holy" and write the meaning here. _____

_____

Now read the following verses: Leviticus 11:44-45; 19:2 and 20:7 and 26. These verses explain even more clearly the main idea of the Book of Leviticus. Explain these verses in your own words below. _____

_____

_____

VOCABULARY

Atonement: to make amends for sin or wrongdoing
Priest: a minister authorized to offer sacrifices
Holy: spiritually pure; sinless
Sacrifice: an offering to God
Sanctified: set apart for a holy purpose
Redemption: to recover or buy back; to make amends for
Contrite: showing remorse or guilt
Transgression: breaking a law or commandment; sin
Iniquity: a wicked act; sin

Why is it that God can never overlook sin?

_____

Those of us who have received Jesus Christ as our Savior are God's chosen people. God wants His chosen people to live a life in close fellowship with Him. We know that before sin entered this world, Adam and Eve had real fellowship with God. After they sinned, they could no longer have fellowship with God because His holiness set Him apart from them. Our sin also sets us apart from fellowship with God. In order that we might be made holy and again have fellowship with God, Jesus Christ offered His own life to pay for our sins.

Four Key Words

The idea of *sacrifice* is a key concept of Leviticus. Three other words are used over and over again. One is the word *holy*, which we have already discussed. It is used 74 times in this book. Another word, *atonement*, is used 56 times. Look up this word and write its definition here. _____

_____

_____

_____

_____

The last important word is the word *blood*, which is used 81 times in this book. If we first understand that the Old Testament sacrifices are a type or picture of what Jesus Christ was one day to do on the cross, why would the word "blood" then be so important in this book? _____

_____

_____

_____

_____

_____

Now list the four key words in the Book of Leviticus: _____

_____

The Sacrificial Offerings

Leviticus taught the Hebrews all the details of the law of God that they were to follow until the Messiah, Jesus Christ, would come and be the eternal sacrifice. We are going to look at five different kinds of sacrificial offerings that pointed to Christ.

■ The first offering is described in Leviticus 1:3. It was a _____ offering. This offering could be any type of animal, but it had to be a _____ without _____.

In what way does this teach us of Christ?

_____

_____

_____

_____

■ The second offering was a grain offering, which was a picture of the life Christ lived on earth. There was no blood shed in this offering. The grain represents a life of service to the Lord.

■ The third offering is described in Leviticus 3:1. It was a _____ offering. This offering could be either a _____ or a _____, but it had to be without _____. This shows that anyone can have peace and fellowship with God. Who is it that has made peace with God for us? _____

■ The fourth offering shows an acknowledgment of sin (the sin offering). God holds us accountable for our sin. Before Christ died for our sin, a person in the Old Testament had to "bring to the Lord _____

_____

as a sin offering" (4:3).

■ The last offering was for acts of sin done against another person and thus against God. This offering, called the guilt offering, shows that no sin can be overlooked. Sometimes people think that if they do the best they can, God will overlook their sins. But God cannot overlook any sin, even if "a person...sins _____

in regard to any of the Lord's _____

_____, he is to bring...a

_____ from the flock, one without

_____" (5:15). Sin against another person is really a sin against

_____.

* * * * * *

Now list the five types of sacrificial offerings in the Book of Leviticus.

✔ _____ Offering

✔ _____ Offering

✔ _____ Offering

✔ _____ Offering

✔ _____ Offering

Jesus Christ, Our High Priest

In Leviticus we are also told about the important work of the priest. The priests had charge of the sacrifices. There are hundreds of interesting things to learn about priests; the important thing to know, however, is that it was the priest who brought the blood to the altar of God to cover the sins of the people. Each priest provided a picture of the Great Sacrifice of Christ for our sins.

LIFE PRINCIPLE: Since the death of Christ on the cross, He is both our Sacrifice and our Priest. He fulfilled all of the Old Testament laws.

As our priest, Christ brought the sacrifice for sin to God. As the sacrifice, He paid the price for sin. From each of the following verses, tell what the New Testament says about these things.

Hebrews 4:14 _____

_____

Hebrews 9:12 _____

_____

Hebrews 9:14 _____

_____

Hebrews 10:4 _____

_____

Hebrews 10:12 _____

_____

Old Testament Understanding Of New Testament Truth

We wonder if people of the Old Testament understood that the sacrifices they were required to make did not really take away their sin but only pictured what Jesus Christ would one day do for all of us. There are many verses in the Old Testament that show that God made this clear to them. Look up the following verses and explain in your own words how God explained this truth.

* * * * * *

1 Samuel 15:22 _____

_____

Psalm 51:16-17 _____

_____

_____

Isaiah 53:5 _____

_____

_____

Conquering The Enemy

Why do we no longer need to sacrifice bulls and goats as they did in the Old Testament?

_____

_____

Why do we no longer need a priest to make sacrifices for us? _____

_____

Use the four key words in the Book of Leviticus that we discussed earlier in our lesson in a paragraph to explain how our sins are cleansed since the New Testament was given.

_____

_____

_____

_____

_____

_____

Have you personally accepted Jesus Christ's sacrifice for your sins and received atonement? _____

11
GOD'S CONCERN FOR ORDER

As the Book of Numbers opens, we see 3,000,000 Israelites in the desert. There is nothing to eat and no water to drink. How were they to live? God was there. He would take care of everything.

God's Concern For Each Person

A principle that helps us to better understand what God is like is His concern for order and detail. Order is heaven's first law. How do we see God's concern for order and detail in the story of creation? _____

_____

_____

_____

_____

_____

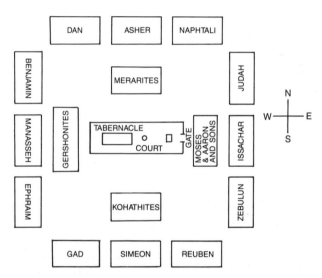

Notice Numbers 1-2, and you will see that God was very interested in each person. The people were divided into twelve tribes. In Numbers 1:2 and 19, what did God command Moses to do? _____

_____

_____

Since order and detail are so important to God, we can understand why God was so concerned about numbering His people. He also arranged the tribes, chose particular men to be priests and assigned certain duties to the people.

Notice the diagram of the twelve tribes of Israel. Read Numbers 1:5-15. Whose names had now become the names of the twelve

---

VOCABULARY

Leprosy: a disease of the skin tissues and nerves characterized by noticeable ulcers and deformities. In the Bible, leprosy is a type of sin.

Manna: a type of food miraculously provided by God for the Israelites in the wilderness

tribes? _____

_____

_____

_____

As you look over chapter 2, what is the main idea of this chapter? _____

_____

Even today, God knows by name all that are His. Copy the part of the following verses that tells you this.

Luke 10:20 _____

_____

Luke 12:7 _____

_____

Philippians 4:23 _____

_____

2 Timothy 2:19 _____

_____

God Meets The People's Needs

Refer back to Exodus and see how God began to meet the needs of the Israelites at the first part of their journey.

EXODUS	CRIES OF THE PEOPLE	NEED MET BY GOD
15:23-27		
16:3, 12-15		
17:2-6		

What was the general attitude of the people in each of these instances? _____

_____

_____

God had provided everything the people would need for the time they would be in the desert. Remember, it was not God's plan for this period to last very long. It was God's plan that His people would soon be in the Promised Land of Canaan where there would be varieties of food and plenty

54

of water to drink. The manna was only to meet the immediate needs of the people, and they should have been grateful for God's provision.

The Results Of A Complaining Spirit

In Numbers 11 and 12, we see more instances of the sin of complaining even by those who were close to Moses.

NUMBERS	WHO COMPLAINED AND WHY?	THE RESULT
11:1, 4-6, 16-20, 31-33		
12:1-2, 9-10		

Conquering The Enemy

God had to take care of 3,000,000 people in the wilderness. Without order and duties for everyone, they could not live. This is why God wants the things of your life to be done "in a fitting and orderly way." He wants you to be successful in what you do.

List some things in your own life that need to be done "in a fitting and orderly way." Give examples for each area below.

* * * * * *

I NEED TO BE ORDERLY ABOUT....

■ Studying God's Word _____

_____

_____

■ My chores _____

_____

_____

■ My homework _____

_____

_____

■ My room _____

_____

_____

In this lesson, we saw how the Israelites sinned by complaining against Moses and God. When we consider how much God had done for them, it is difficult to understand why they grumbled and complained so much. But before you exclaim how terrible the Israelites were, ask yourself the following questions.

• Do I complain very much during the day about the work my teacher gives me to do? _____

• Do I complain to my parents about my chores and things I am asked to do for them? _____

• Do I complain to my friends that things are not done fairly? _____

• Are there other things I complain about? _____

• Am I showing that I am not satisfied with what God is doing for me and the things He has given me in my life in order that I might mature? _____

> LIFE PRINCIPLE: When the sin of a complaining attitude comes into your life, realize how foolish you are and tell the Lord that you are sorry.

A complaining attitude does not help the situation but only leads to misery. Like all other sins it keeps us from being what God wants us to be. God does not want sin to keep us unhappy on the inside. He wants us to have a joyful spirit—and we can, if we learn to be thankful to Him instead of constantly complaining.

12 DESERT WANDERINGS

Do you remember when we studied the story of Abraham? God called him to be the father of a great nation. God made a promise to the Hebrew nation through Abraham. What was this promise? See Genesis 12:1-3.

_____

_____

_____

_____

_____

God's Goal For Israel: The Promised Land

Even during the 400 years of slavery in Egypt, God did not forget His promise to Abraham and to His people. When He brought the people out of Egypt, He intended that they return to this land of promise, Canaan. Now that He had organized His people and had met their needs thus far, God wanted to bring them to Canaan. With this in mind, what did God

---

VOCABULARY

Rebellion: defiance of authority
Divination: the practice of trying to foretell the future or the unknown

---

tell Moses to do now? (Numbers 13:1-2, 17)

_____

_____

_____

_____

Now read Numbers 13:18-20. God gave these men specific things for which they were to look. List six things they were to take note of.

🗸 _____

🗸 _____

🗸 _____

🗸 _____

🗸 _____

🗸 _____

The people were anxious because they had been wandering in the desert for almost two years, and now it was time to go into the Promised Land. Read Numbers 13:2 again. God said to "explore the land of Canaan, which I am _____ to the Israelites." This means that they didn't have to worry—the land was already theirs. God just wanted them to search out the land before they took possession.

The Spies Give Their Report

Study Numbers 13:25-14:2 and fill in the

blanks to find out what the spies reported.

The spies returned to Moses from exploring the land after _____ days. They reported that the cities were _____ and very _____.

_____ said that the people should go up and take possession of the land. Caleb said the Hebrews could certainly do it; but the other spies (except for Joshua) said not to attack those people, for they were _____.
They said the people there were of great _____, and the Hebrews seemed like _____.

Now, the people were upset at God for bringing them to this land. Joshua and Caleb tried to talk to the people of Israel. In Numbers 14:7-11, it says they thought the land was "_____."
They said, "If the Lord is _____ with us, he will _____ us into that land, a land flowing with _____ and _____, and will _____ it to us. Only do not _____ against the Lord. And do not be _____ of the people of the land....But the whole _____ talked about _____ them."

Then God was grieved because the people refused to _____ Him for all the miraculous _____ which He had performed among them.

God Punishes Unbelief

God had tried again and again through many signs and miracles and with great patience to teach the people to trust Him. But again and again they rebelled against His provision and His teachings. Finally, because they would not believe that He had given them the land of Canaan to possess and enjoy, God made a decision. What was this decision? Read Numbers 14:22-24 and 29-35. _____

_____

_____

_____

_____

_____

_____

_____

_____

Thus, only Joshua and Caleb, the two spies who had given a favorable report showing trust in God, would be allowed to go into the Promised Land. They alone believed God.

Conquering The Enemy

LIFE PRINCIPLE: The Bible says that "rebellion is like the sin of divination."

God wants us to realize how terrible the sin of rebellion is. The Hebrews rebelled against God by not trusting Him and taking possession of the land. Yet they would not realize their sin and repent of it. If they had, God would have forgiven them and let them into the land of promise.

This is an area with which many young people have problems. Are there areas of rebellion in your life that keep you from having the blessings of God? If there are, name them here and confess them before the Lord. _____

_____

_____

_____

_____

_____

_____

Rebellion kept the Israelites from trusting God. Faith in the promises of God is a key to victory as a Christian. Name one problem that you are presently having and write out a verse containing a promise that will help you trust God in this area.

_____

_____

_____

_____

_____

_____

_____

_____

_____

13 MOSES' FINAL CHARGE

The Israelites wanted their own way again and again and would not simply obey God. Thus, they missed out on all the blessings God wanted them to have. And instead, they were punished for their sin and not allowed to enter the land of promise. Because of their disobedience, forty more years would go by before anyone would enter Canaan.

Deuteronomy means "second law." This book was written at the end of the forty years of wandering just before Moses died. In the book Moses again instructs the people concerning the need to obey God. He tells of the blessings they would receive if they would only trust and obey Him.

Moses' Final Command: Obey The Lord

How does Deuteronomy 4:31 describe the Lord? _____

_____

According to this verse, because He is merciful, what three things will He not do to Israel?

🖝 _____

🖝 _____

🖝 _____

VOCABULARY

Merciful: not allowing harm to come to an offender; kind and compassionate treatment; a forgiving attitude

---

Therefore, we see that God does not want any evil to come into our lives, and He will do all He can to show patience to us while we learn. But He does want us to listen to God's Word as Moses explains in Deuteronomy 5:1. Finish the command that Moses gave: "Hear, O Israel, the decrees and laws I declare in your hearing today.

_____

_____

_____

_____

_____."

Now read Deuteronomy 6 carefully and list at least five commands that are still important to each of us today.

- _____
- _____
- _____
  _____
- _____
- _____
- _____
- _____
- _____
- _____

Obedience Is For Our Good

LIFE PRINCIPLE: It is important to learn that obedience to rules and authority is really for our own good.

So often we obey because we must or because we want to avoid being disciplined. How much better it is to realize that God always has our best in mind! Obeying God will allow Him to give us all the blessings He desires to give.

Moses continues to talk to the people. He reminds them of why they were made to wander in the desert for forty years. What was the reason as given in Deuteronomy 8:2? _____

_____

_____

_____

Why had God not been able to bless the people as He desired? See Deuteronomy 9:24. _____

_____

_____

Then Moses gives the people many reasons for obeying God. Read the following verses and write the reason given in each verse. Notice that these can also be taken as promises from God to His people.

■ Deuteronomy 20:4 _____

_____

■ Deuteronomy 28:8 _____

_____

■ Deuteronomy 31:6 _____

_____

Puzzle

Using the code below, fill in the following blanks to find out what one of God's purposes was for the people of Israel.

A = 26	H = 19	O = 12	U = 6
B = 25	I = 18	P = 11	V = 5
C = 24	J = 17	Q = 10	W = 4
D = 23	K = 16	R = 9	X = 3
E = 22	L = 15	S = 8	Y = 2
F = 21	M = 14	T = 7	Z = 1
G = 20	N = 13		

"... ___ ___ ___ ___ ___ ___ ___ ___ ___ ___
      2 12 6   4 18 15 15   25 22   26

___ ___ ___ ___ ___ ___ ___ ___ ___ ___ ___ ___ ___ ___ ___
11 22 12 11 15 22   19 12 15 2   7 12   7 19 22

___ ___ ___ ___ ___ ___ ___ ___ ___ ___ ___ "
15 12   9 23   2 12   6   9   20 12 23

(___ ___ ___ ___ ___ ___ ___ ___ ___ ___ ___ ___:___).
 23 22   6   7 22   9 12 13 12 14   2   A   H

The Death Of Moses

After Moses finished his sermon, God gave him a special vision. What did God allow Moses to see in Deuteronomy 34:1-4? _____

_____

_____

Thus, before Moses died, God showed him all the land which had been promised to Abraham. And so Moses died at the age of 120 years and was buried by God in a secret place. A great tribute was written about Moses in Deuteronomy 34:10. Joshua probably wrote these words: "_____

_____

_____

_____."

Key Places In The Israelites' Travels

Using the maps in your Bible, find and label the following important places. To help you, they are marked by dots on the map below.

- Rameses—a city the Israelites built for Pharaoh
- Marah—the bitter waters were made sweet
- Elim—the Lord provided twelve springs of water
- Rephidim—the Israelites defeated the Amalekites
- Mount Sinai—God gave the law to Moses
- Kadesh Barnea—spies sent and then returned with their report
- Mount Nebo—Moses saw the Promised Land before his death
- Jericho—the first city in Canaan conquered by the Israelites

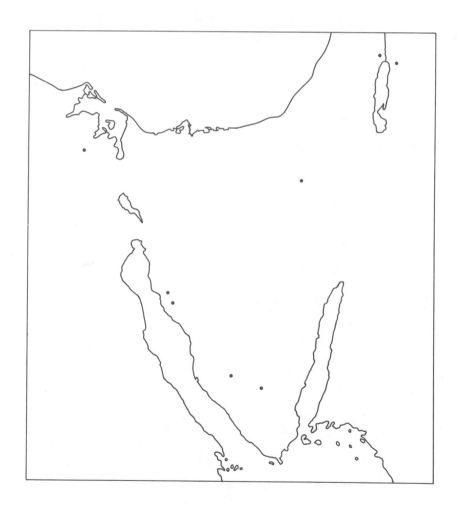

Conquering The Enemy

We have studied how important it was for the Israelites to learn to trust and obey God. Why is it also in your best interest to obey the laws and authorities God has placed in your life? _____

_____

_____

_____

_____

Give an example of a time when it was better for you to obey than disobey.

_____

_____

_____

_____

_____

Be honest! Do you often have a rebellious attitude, or do you obey because you know it is best for you? _____

_____

14 VICTORY IN CANAAN

Israel Gets A New Leader

Now that Moses had died, God transferred the leadership to Joshua. Remember, Joshua had seen God's miracles in Egypt. He had been one of the spies that had entered Canaan and given a good report. He had patiently waited through forty years of wandering in the desert to be able to enter the Promised Land. Now, instead of fear, there was great joy and hope as they all prepared to conquer Canaan. What did God tell Joshua to do, and what promise did He give to Joshua and the people? See Joshua 1:1-3. _____

_____

_____

_____

_____

_____

_____

_____

_____

When God gives us a commandment, He always gives us promises to help us. And God always keeps His promises. Read Joshua 1:5-9. List the things God asked Joshua to do on the left and the promises for obedience on the right.

GOD'S COMMANDS	GOD'S PROMISES

Joshua now gives a command to the people. What was the command? (Joshua 1:11)

_____

_____

_____

_____

_____

_____

How did the people respond in verse 16?

_____

_____

_____

How had the attitude of this generation of people changed from those of their parents? _____

_____

_____

_____

_____

Entering The Land

Now the people of Canaan were wicked and idolatrous people. God had warned them in the destruction of Sodom and Gomorrah, but they had not turned from their evil ways. Now God was going to destroy their power and give their land to the Israelites.

Just as Moses had sent spies into Canaan forty years earlier, Joshua again sent two spies into the land to bring back a report. What report was brought back this time? See Joshua 2:23-24. _____

_____

_____

_____

_____

_____

Before they could enter the land, they had to cross the great river Jordan. God was ready to use signs and miracles again to give victory to His people. Read Joshua 3:13-17. How did God enable the people to cross the Jordan River? _____

_____

_____

_____

_____

Victory At Jericho

LIFE PRINCIPLE: Remember that victory comes from obeying God's commands and trusting in His promises.

The first city that had to be conquered was the great walled city of Jericho. In the victory over the city of Jericho, the Israelites had to do both these things (obey and trust God). Read Joshua 6:1-21.

■ What commands did the people have to obey? (What did God ask them to do?) ____
_____
_____
_____

■ What promises did they have to trust God to accomplish? _____
_____
_____
_____
_____
_____

Sin Brings Defeat

The next city that was to be conquered was Ai, which was also a strong, walled city. But it was no stronger than Jericho had been and should have fallen just as easily. Joshua sent about 3,000 men to Ai, but they were driven back and thirty-six were killed. In Joshua 7:6-9, Joshua is grieved and does not understand why they were defeated. Why had God allowed this to happen? Then God told Joshua the reason. Find out what had happened in Joshua 7:10-11.

_____

_____

_____

_____

_____

God then told Joshua that when there was sin among the people, they would not have victory. He told Joshua how to find the sinner and how to deal with the sin. So Joshua began to go through the camp until finally, God pointed out that it was Achan who had sinned. What did Achan do, and what was his punishment? (Joshua 7:19-25)

_____

_____

_____

_____

Joshua and the Israelites now went again and ambushed the people of the city of Ai. All the people were killed, and the city was burned completely to the ground. Again and again, in city after city, Joshua and the Israelites conquered the rest of the land of Canaan. Again and again they had to obey God and trust Him for the victories. What had God given the people as explained in Joshua 24:13? _____

_____

_____

Settling The Land

Now that the Israelites had conquered their enemies in the land, it was time for them to settle down and make their homes in Canaan. Rather than everyone settling down and living in the same place, they needed to spread themselves throughout the land to make sure that all the land was constantly in the possession of the Israelites and not the Canaanites. Thus in chapters 13-21, Joshua divided the land among the tribes of Israel. Notice the map to see where each tribe settled.

CANAAN DIVIDED AMONG THE TWELVE TRIBES

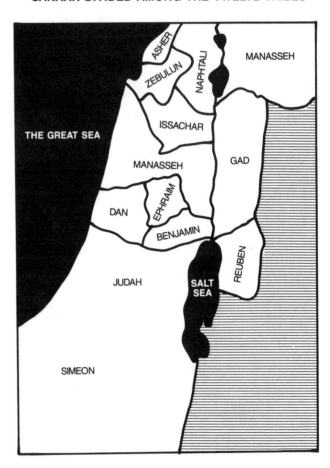

Puzzle

Crossing the Jordan was an important step to victory for the Israelites. Leaving a life of wandering, the Israelites became conquerors through the power of God. Many Old Testament heroes experienced victory through God's power. Use the following clues to name some of these heroes.

1. He did not die because God "took him away."
2. He helped his brother Moses with the Israelites.
3. A slave who became in charge of Egypt
4. He led the Israelites out of Egypt.
5. These people were set free.
6. The lions' mouths were shut against him.
7. He was swallowed by a great fish.
8. He won a battle with 300 men.
9. A godly son of Adam
10. He lived longer than any other man.
11. He returned from Canaan with a good report.
12. He led the Israelites into the Promised Land.
13. His new name became the name of a nation.
14. God promised that he would be the father of a new nation.
15. He killed a giant.
16. He was willing to be sacrificed by his father.
17. He and his family lived through the Flood.

Conquering The Enemy

Read Joshua 24:17-18. The Israelites were reminded of all the things God had done for them. In the box below, make a list of your own of the things God has done for you.

-
-
-
-
-

-
-
-
-
-

Before Joshua died, the people of Israel dwelt in all of the land of Canaan. They made a commitment again to the Lord. What was this commitment as given in Joshua 24:24?

_____

_____

If you are grateful for all the blessings of God and if your attitude is the same as that of the Israelites, write a similar commitment to God in your own words. Make it a prayer from your own heart to Almighty God.

_____

_____

_____

_____

_____

15 SIN AND SUFFERING

The story of the period of the judges is often like the story of our lives. The Israelites were finally in the Promised Land, and God had given them victory over the inhabitants of the land. But over and over again, the people turned away from God. And whenever they turned away, trouble and problems resulted. Then they would ask God to help them. Again and again God would show mercy and bring them out of their troubles. But just as soon as things seemed "okay," they turned away from God again. Read Judges 17:6. What was the problem? _____

_____

_____

_____

This is one of the key ideas of the Book of Judges. It explains why the people of Israel had problems again and again.

God wanted the Israelites to remember they were set apart in a special way. He wants you to remember the same thing. But, as you will see, seven times Israel was in bondage to another nation; and seven times God delivered them. As you read about each of these times, let the lives of the Israelites remind you of your own life, and see if you fall into the same cycle.

Oppression And Deliverance

The Book of Judges gets its name from the people chosen by God to deliver the people from bondage to other nations each time they turned back to God. It was God's desire that Israel not live in bondage but allow God Himself to rule their lives. As you will see in this lesson, the following pattern kept repeating itself throughout the Book of Judges.

★ Falling into sin
★ Servitude
★ Repentance
★ Deliverance

As the title to this lesson indicates, sin always brings suffering in the lives of God's people. And as the children of Israel saw, deliverance can only come as we turn from our sins and return to the Lord. Read the following verses in the Book of Judges and answer the questions.

VOCABULARY

Oppression: to be burdened down
Repentance: to feel such regret over sin that you turn from wrongdoing
Servitude: slavery
Sanctify: set apart for a special purpose

THE FIRST OPPRESSION

3:7—What was Israel's attitude toward God? _____

_____

3:8—What was the result? _____

3:9—Whom did God use to deliver them? _____

THE SECOND OPPRESSION

3:12—Israel's attitude _____

3:14—Results _____

_____

_____

3:15—The judge God used to deliver them _____

THE THIRD OPPRESSION

3:31—The judge God used to slay 600 Philistines _____

THE FOURTH OPPRESSION

4:1—Israel's attitude _____

_____

4:2-3—Results _____

_____

4:4-6—The two judges God used to deliver them _____

_____

THE FIFTH OPPRESSION

6:1—Israel's attitude _____

_____

6:6—Results _____

_____

_____

7:14—The judge God used _____

THE SIXTH OPPRESSION

8:33-34—Israel's attitude _____

_____

10:1-3—Judges God used _____

THE SEVENTH OPPRESSION

10:6—Israel's attitude _____

_____

10:7—Results _____

_____

10:10-14—How did God feel this time? _____

_____

_____

11:11—Deliverer _____

THE EIGHTH OPPRESSION

12:8, 11, 13—Who were three other judges God used? _____

_____

THE NINTH OPPRESSION

13:1—Israel's attitude _____

_____

13:1—Result _____

_____

15:16-20—Deliverer _____

Now look at the last verse in the Book of Judges. Even after the Lord had delivered them many times, what attitude did the people have once again? _____

_____

The Story Of Gideon

Read the following verses from the Book of Judges and complete the statements to learn more about the story of Gideon. Then unscramble the circled letters to form a word that shows how God used Gideon.

- Gideon was the son of ___ ___ ___ ___ ___ (6:11).
- Gideon was trying to hide his wheat from the ___ ___ ◯ ___ ___ ___ ___ ___ ___ (6:11).
- God saw Gideon as a mighty ___ ___ ___ ___ ___ ___ ___ (6:12).
- Gideon saw the ___ ___ ___ ◯ ___ of the Lord face to face (6:22).
- Gideon used a wool ___ ◯ ___ ___ ___ ___ to make certain God would ___ ___ ◯ ___ Israel by His hand (6:37).
- Anyone who trembled with ___ ___ ___ ___ was told to go home; this left 10,000 men (7:3).
- But the Lord said, "There are still ___ ___ ___ ___ ___ ___ ___ men" (7:4).
- God told Gideon to send away all those who lapped water with their ___ ___ ___ ___ ___ ◯ ___ (7:5). Then He said that it would be by these remaining three ___ ___ ___ ___ ◯ ___ ___ men that He would deliver the Midianites into Gideon's hand (7:7).
- Gideon's men blew their ___ ◯ ___ ___ ___ ___ ___ ___ and shouted, "For the ___ ___ ___ ___ and for ___ ◯ ___ ___ ___ ___" (7:18).
- When this happened, the Midianites cried out and ___ ___ ◯ ___ (7:21).
- Thus God ___ ___ ___ ___ the Midianites into their hands (8:3).

Unscrambled word— ___ ___ ___ ___ ___ ___ ___ ___ ___

Conquering The Enemy

Look up the word "sanctified" and write its meaning here._____

_____

God wanted the Israelites to realize they had been "set apart." You also have been set apart by God for a special purpose. Do you, however, like the Israelites, forget about God sometimes and do "what you see fit"? _____

What can you learn about the hearts of men from the Book of Judges? _____

_____

_____

What can you do to keep the same pattern from occurring in your own life? _____

_____

_____

_____

16
THE STORY OF RUTH

The story of Ruth takes place during the same time as the first events in the Book of Judges. All through the Old Testament we are seeing evidences of Jesus Christ. God had promised that Christ would be born through the lineage of Abraham down through David. And Ruth was David's great-grandmother. So you can see that this woman had an important place in God's plan for the coming of Christ.

Let's learn what kind of woman she was to be used in such a special way. Begin reading the first chapter of Ruth to find out the following.

► The story of Ruth begins with another woman named Naomi. Why did Naomi's family leave the land of God's people,

Canaan? (1:1) _____

_____

_____

_____

► Naomi's sons married heathen girls from Moab. What is a heathen? _____

_____

► Naomi's husband and both her sons died. Naomi decided to return to the land of her people in Canaan. When she returned, which one of her daughters-in-law went with her? (1:14-16) _____

► Did Ruth turn to the true God? (1:16)

_____

► To which town did they return? (1:19)

_____

What was God's future plan for this town?

_____

_____

Though she was once a heathen, Ruth gave her life to God; and the Lord graciously blessed her life. She married a fine man and was used of God in the lineage of His Son.

Conquering The Enemy

You need to make the same decision Ruth made—to turn your life completely over to the Lord. Be honest! Have you truly turned your life and your attitudes over to God? Ask yourself the questions below. Your honest answers will help you know whether you have really committed yourself to Christ or whether you are just doing things which look good or must be done out of duty.

• Have I trusted Jesus Christ as my Lord and Savior?	Yes	No
• Do I enjoy Sunday school and church?	Yes	No
• Am I eager to learn more about Christ?	Yes	No
• Do I read my Bible on my own?	Yes	No
• Do I really try to do what God says?	Yes	No
• When I sin, am I immediately sorry?	Yes	No
• When I sin, do I confess it to the Lord?	Yes	No
• Do I do my best in school to please God?	Yes	No
• Do I honor and obey my parents?	Yes	No
• Do I tell the Lord Jesus I love Him?	Yes	No

Review

Complete the following exercises to help you review the material we have already studied. Fill in the chart to show the lineage of Adam.

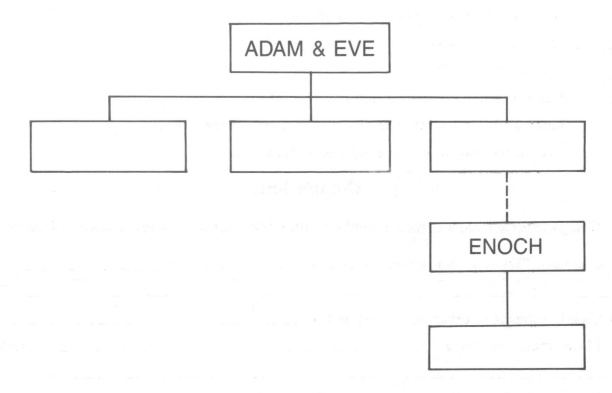

Matching

Match the following items.

_____ 1. Blamed his wife for his sin

_____ 2. Did not die because God took him away

_____ 3. Killed his brother

_____ 4. Clothed Adam and Eve with garments of skin

_____ 5. Lived the longest on the earth

_____ 6. Built an ark that is a type of Christ

_____ 7. Gave an offering acceptable to God

_____ 8. Was deceived

_____ 9. Began a new spiritual lineage

_____10. Was pictured in the Old Testament

A. Seth

B. Jesus

C. Cain

D. Enoch

E. Eve

F. Methuselah

G. God

H. Abel

I. Adam

J. Noah

Putting Things In Order

Number the following in the order in which they occurred.

_____ Eve is deceived by Satan.

_____ Adam and Eve enjoy the Garden of Eden.

_____ The world is created.

_____ Cain kills his brother.

_____ Adam and Eve are fearful and full of guilt.

_____ Adam and Eve are told they must work hard on the earth.

_____ God clothes Adam and Eve with skins from animals.

Completion

Complete these sentences with a word or phrase from our lessons on the Book of Genesis.

• God said, "You will surely die." Satan said, _____

_____."

• Creation means to bring into being out of _____.

• Three results of sin are _____, _____ and

_____ .

• God promised to build a great nation through the descendants of _____.

• The binding agreement given by God to Abraham was called a _____.

• Abraham wanted his son, _____, to have a _____ from his own people, so he sent his trusted _____ to find a _____ for _____.

• Jacob deceived Esau and stole the _____ and the _____.

• The twelve sons of Jacob became the twelve _____ _____ .

• Jacob's name was changed to the name of a new nation, _____.

• Jacob's son who became a ruler in Egypt was _____.

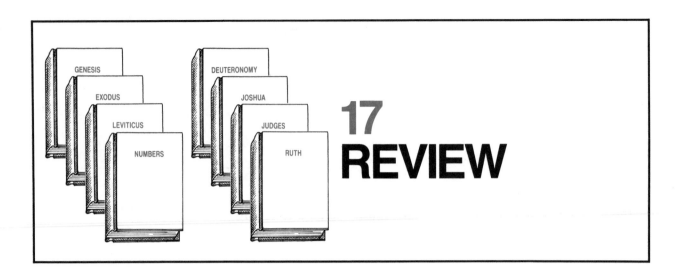

GENESIS

EXODUS

LEVITICUS

NUMBERS

DEUTERONOMY

JOSHUA

JUDGES

RUTH

17 REVIEW

The Lineage Of Abraham

Fill in the names to complete the following chart.

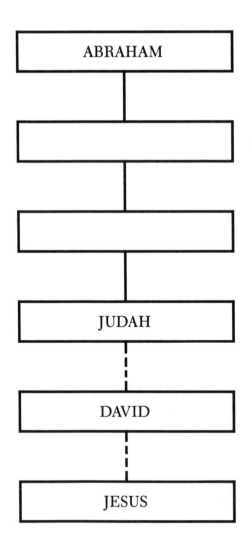

ABRAHAM

JUDAH

DAVID

JESUS

Where Do You Find...

In which book of the Bible do you find the following? Choose from the following books.

GENESIS   EXODUS   LEVITICUS   NUMBERS   DEUTERONOMY

_____ 1. The main theme of "holiness"

_____ 2. Cain and Abel

_____ 3. Moses leading the Israelites out of Egypt

_____ 4. The death of Moses

_____ 5. The story of Noah

_____ 6. The Ten Commandments are given.

_____ 7. Joseph is sold as a slave.

_____ 8. The tabernacle is built.

_____ 9. Isaac and Rebekah

_____ 10. The spies are sent into Canaan.

_____ 11. Jacob and Esau

_____ 12. Bondage in Egypt

_____ 13. Creation

_____ 14. The ten plagues

_____ 15. Five kinds of sacrificial offerings

_____ 16. Adam and Eve

_____ 17. The Passover

_____ 18. God's promise to Abraham

_____ 19. Moses' last sermon

_____ 20. The Israelites are counted.

The Story Of Jacob

Number the following details in the order in which they occurred.

_____ Jacob's mother tells him he must leave home.

_____ Jacob goes to live with Laban.

_____ Jacob's name is changed to Israel.

_____ Jacob marries Leah.

_____ Rachel dies when Benjamin is born.

_____ Jacob steals the birthright.

_____ Rachel becomes Jacob's wife.

_____ Esau welcomes Jacob home.

Name The Book

Match the following items, telling in which book of the Bible each of the following occurs.

_____ 1. The story of Gideon

_____ 2. The death of Moses

_____ 3. The defeat at Ai because of sin

_____ 4. Two spies sent to survey the land

_____ 5. The story of Samson

_____ 6. The Battle of Jericho

_____ 7. Sin, Servitude, Repentance, Deliverance

_____ 8. God's concern for order

_____ 9. Dividing the land among the tribes

_____ 10. The Israelites go into the Promised Land

_____ 11. "Everyone did as he saw fit."

_____ 12. Twelve spies sent to explore the land

A. Numbers

B. Deuteronomy

C. Joshua

D. Judges

The Judges Of Israel

Use the material from Lesson Fifteen to fill in the names of the judges whom God used during each of the following periods of oppression. Remember that in some cases God used two or three judges during the same period.

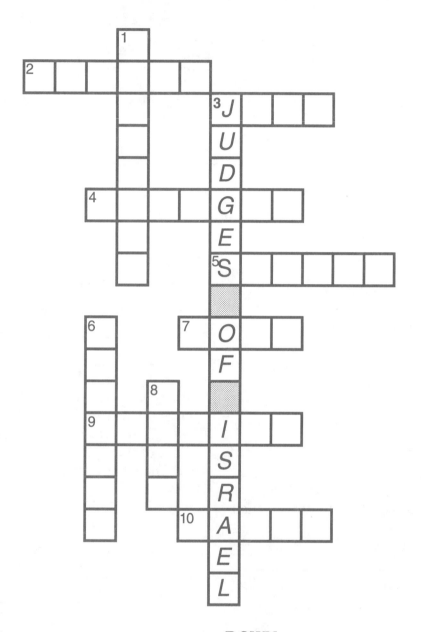

ACROSS:
2. The Fifth Oppression
3. The Sixth Oppression
4. The Third Oppression
5. The Ninth Oppression
7. The Sixth Oppression
9. The First Oppression
10. The Fourth Oppression

DOWN:
1. The Seventh Oppression
6. The Fourth Oppression
8. The Second Oppression

18
SAMUEL—ISRAEL'S LAST JUDGE

Israel Rejects God

The book of 1 Samuel is the story of three men—Samuel, Saul and David. Up until the time of Samuel, judges ruled over the people of Israel. Read 1 Samuel 8:4-8 to learn why Samuel was the last true judge in Israel.

► What did the Israelites ask of Samuel?

_____

_____

_____

► According to verse 7, who wanted to reign over them (guide and direct their lives)? _____

► According to the Lord, whom had the people rejected? _____

► Why did the people want a king? What was their problem? _____

VOCABULARY

Iniquity: breaking a moral law; sin
Routed: to put to disorderly flight or retreat

_____

_____

_____

_____

_____

Even after all the problems in their history that we read about in the Book of Judges, the people still did not desire to serve God. They wanted useless things—things of the world. Read 1 Samuel 12:20-21 and then copy verse 21 here. _____

_____

_____

_____

_____

_____

_____

_____

_____

In chapter 8, God spoke through Samuel to tell the people how wrong it was to desire another ruler besides God. He told them that a king would bring wars and taxes and problems that they had not faced before. What was the people's attitude according to verse 19? _____

_____

_____

The Israelites had chosen the useless things of the world. God had told them that worldly things would eventually harm them, but

the Israelites would not listen to God's warnings. Finally, when they would not listen, what did God tell Samuel? (1 Samuel 8:21-22) _____

_____

_____

It is not always good for us to have everything we want. So sometimes God gives us our way just to teach us this lesson.

The First King Of Israel

When the people of Israel set their minds to have a king, God did not act spitefully against them. God always wants the best for His people. Thus He chose a king that had strong character. Describe this man God had chosen to be the first king over Israel from 1 Samuel 9:1-2.

	THE ATTRIBUTES OF SAUL
HIS FATHER	
HIS APPEARANCE	
HIS CHARACTER	

Samuel: A Man Of Prayer

As we study the life of Samuel, we find that he was truly a man of God. While we know that as all men, Samuel was a sinner, it is difficult to find mistakes in his life. The best explanation for this was that his life was centered around prayer. As you have already seen, Samuel talked to the Lord continually and included Him in all his

plans and activities.

This attitude began when Samuel was a baby. Even his birth was prayed for by his mother, Hannah. What did she ask of the Lord? (1 Samuel 1:10-11) _____

_____

_____

When Samuel was young, his mother kept her promise and took him to live at the house of the Lord in Shiloh. Thus, as a child, Samuel ministered to the priest, Eli. Samuel learned early to listen to the Lord and was a child of prayer. Explain how Samuel learned to hear the voice of the Lord from 1 Samuel 3:3-10. _____

_____

_____

_____

_____

_____

_____

_____

As a judge of Israel, Samuel brought victory to his people through prayer. Read 1 Samuel 7:8-10 and explain what happened when Samuel prayed. _____

_____

_____

_____

_____

We have already studied how the people rejected God by asking for a king. What was the first thing that Samuel did when this happened? (1 Samuel 8:6) _____

_____

LIFE PRINCIPLE:

Prayer is not...
• A good luck charm to prevent misfortune from coming into our lives
• A tool to use when we are in an emergency situation
• A way to get our selfish desires met
• Something memorized and repeated without thinking

Prayer is...
• The Christian's way of talking to our Father about our problems and feelings
• A time to listen to direction and guidance from our Father
• A time to praise God and show Him reverence
• Answered according to God's will with our best in mind

Success In Prayer

There are principles for success in God's Word, and this is true of success in prayer also. There are certain areas that will hinder our prayer relationship with God, and there are principles that God will honor.

After each verse below, name the quality that is being discussed: stubbornness, a clear conscience, a yielded heart, obedience, selfishness, sin, a humble spirit or disobedience.

CONDITIONS FOR PRAYER	HINDRANCES TO PRAYER
2 Chronicles 7:14—	1 Samuel 13:13; 14:36-37—
Jeremiah 29:13—	Psalm 66:18—
James 5:16—	Zechariah 7:12-13—
1 John 3:22—	James 4:3—

Samuel grieved because the Israelites had chosen to reject God and have a worldly king rule them. But even at this time, what was his attitude as seen in 1 Samuel 12:23?

_____

_____

Conquering The Enemy

We discussed two very important areas of your life in this lesson.

The first area is that of getting involved in useless things—things of the world that will eventually harm you. Think about your own life and consider areas of your life that God may want you to think about leaving alone. List these things here.

_____

_____

_____

_____

The second area is the area of prayer. One of the key reasons you need to have good communication with God is so that you will know what God wants you to do and not do in your life. God wants to make your life go well, and He will always guide you in the best direction if you listen to Him as Samuel learned to do. Now think about your own prayer life.
• Do you pray to God every day? _____
• Name one or two problems that you have that you need to discuss with the Lord today. _____

_____

_____

• Name one or two things that you have to be particularly grateful for today. _____

_____

Go to the Lord in prayer now and thank Him for these things.

19
SAUL— ISRAEL'S FIRST KING

As we learned in our last lesson, Saul became the first king of Israel. Do you think Saul was a good choice to be king over Israel? _____ Why or why not?

_____

_____

_____

_____

_____

Saul was very tall, and all of the people admired him. They were happy with their new king. Samuel was still close to God in prayer and still told the people God's wishes. One day, Samuel said to Saul, "The people of Amalek are wicked. They must be punished. God will send you to punish them. You must destroy them and everything that they have."

VOCABULARY

Anoint: to put oil on when a person is dedicated to be set apart for a holy purpose or calling
Divination: witchcraft
Heed: to pay close attention to

Saul had a large army; and they destroyed the city, but they did not destroy everything. They took the best sheep, the best lambs and the other things that they wanted. That night, God spoke to Samuel and told him Saul had disobeyed. Samuel was very sorry and could not sleep but prayed to God all night long. When Samuel asked Saul about this, he gave the excuse that they were saving the best to offer to God upon the altar. Samuel just shook his head in sorrow, for he knew Saul had greatly sinned by not obeying God.

Obedience Is #1 With God

Study 1 Samuel 15:22-23 and answer the following questions to see how God felt about Saul's actions.
• Saul made sacrifices to the Lord of what he had taken. What does God say is better than sacrifice? _____
• What is better than the fat of rams?

_____

• How does He describe rebellion? _____

_____

• How does He describe arrogance?

_____

• Why did God reject Saul from being king? _____

_____

LIFE PRINCIPLE: God will reject a rebellious heart.

Time For A New King

The Lord now asked Samuel to anoint a new king from among the sons of Jesse. Jesse brought out all of his sons before Samuel. But God told Samuel that none of them was the one He had chosen. All of Jesse's sons looked like strong, capable men, but how did God choose the leader He wanted? (1 Samuel 16:7) _____

_____

_____

Then Jesse brought forward his youngest son, David. What did the Lord immediately tell Samuel? (1 Samuel 16:12-13)

_____

_____

_____

So Samuel anointed David, and "the _____ of the _____ came upon David in power" (1 Samuel 16:13).

David And Goliath

David had been anointed by God to be the next king of Israel, but Saul was still the king. David would have to wait for God's

timing. For now, David would go to the king's court and play the harp before Saul, who was constantly troubled by an evil spirit. His music would soothe Saul and make him feel better.

During this time, the Israelites were in battle against the Philistines. From reading 1 Samuel 17, draw lines to match the following parts of each sentence to tell the story of David and Goliath.

All the men of Israel

The man who killed Goliath

Goliath made fun

David believed that God

Saul wanted David

David took only

When they saw Goliath was dead

David slew Goliath

would deliver him.

a sling and five smooth stones.

the Philistines turned and ran.

were afraid of Goliath.

with one shot of his sling.

to wear his armor.

would receive great wealth.

of David when he saw him coming.

A Heart Of Jealousy

All of Israel celebrated because of the death of their great foe. There was singing and celebration, and David immediately became the hero of Israel. After Saul heard his people singing greater praises to David than to himself, Saul began to be jealous of David. Saul was allowing an evil spirit to gain more and more control of his heart. The jealousy began to grow, and very soon, Saul had a deep hatred for David. Saul came to hate David so much that he wanted him killed. Describe what Saul tried to do in the following verses.

1 Samuel 18:10-11 _____

_____

_____

1 Samuel 19:10 _____

_____

1 Samuel 19:15 _____

_____

_____

Conquering The Enemy

Think about the following verse and how it applied to David.

> *Fear of man will prove to be a snare, but whoever trusts in the Lord is kept safe.*
> Proverbs 29:25

Can you apply this verse to a situation in your own life? Write about a situation in which you were afraid, but God gave you the courage you needed. _____

_____

_____

| JEALOUSY ⟶ HATRED ⟶ MURDER |

The above pattern was the basic problem in Saul's life. You surely would not be guilty of murder; but Christ said that when you have hatred in your heart, it is as bad as murder. You should ask God to keep the spirit of jealousy and hatred out of your heart and to fill your heart with love for others.

20 THE CHARACTER OF DAVID

Even though God had chosen and anointed David to be the next king of Israel, it was not time for a new king to be crowned. David had to patiently wait for God's timing. As the jealousy and hatred of Saul grew stronger and stronger, David had to learn to walk in the strength of the Lord. God wants you to learn this same lesson.

Saul continued to make attacks on David's life. David had the right attitude and realized that Saul was still king and was still the authority over him. He wanted to be obedient and submissive to this authority even if the authority was wrong in his actions. Copy what the Bible says about David's behavior and attitude from 1 Samuel 18:14. _____

_____

_____

_____

_____

Jonathan: A True Friend

God also established a very unique friendship between two young men who we would normally assume would be enemies. Jonathan was the son of King Saul. Normally, he would have been in line to become king when his father died; and since David had been chosen to become the next king, we would think that Jonathan and David would be rivals, not friends. But in 1 Samuel 18:1, we see that God had established a very special love between Jonathan and David. What phrases explain this friendship? _____

_____

_____

_____

_____

_____

When Jonathan realized that his father, King Saul, was trying to kill David, what did he do? (1 Samuel 19:1-2) _____

_____

_____

_____

_____

Then, in verse 4, how did he try to reason with his father? _____

_____

_____

_____

King Saul, however, hated David and would not change. Later, when Jonathan again defended David, what did Saul do? (1 Samuel 20:32-33) _____

_____

_____

_____

_____

_____

Thus, Jonathan grieved for David and warned him to stay away; for Saul would not rest until David was killed. The concern and love shown by Jonathan for his friend is even more remarkable when we remind ourselves that he knew David would be the next king instead of himself. God's love can cover any situation if we allow it to.

Returning Love For Hate

Thus, because of Saul, David had to flee for his life. David and his men hid in caves and other such places. Saul came after David with soldiers who were ready to kill David as soon as they found him.

These were very hard days for David. He did not have a home. He could not be with his family. He knew Saul would kill him if he had the chance. But God had a purpose for what was happening even during such tribulations. God was preparing David to be

the right kind of king. He learned how to handle himself. He learned how to work with other men. He learned how to handle problems God's way and have courage. Most important, he learned to trust God, not men.

Instead of letting Saul's hatred harden his heart, David returned love for hate. Twice David had the opportunity to kill Saul but did not do it. Read all of 1 Samuel 24 and complete the following sentences to learn about one of these times.

94

- Saul went after David with _____.
- Saul came to the cave where David was staying. He went inside to rest, and David

_____ .
- David could have killed Saul while he was sleeping but instead he cut off _____

_____ .
- David would not let his men attack Saul because he was _____

_____ .
- After Saul awoke and left, David called after him. He showed him the piece of his robe and said that others thought he should kill Saul, but he couldn't kill God's anointed. He told Saul that the Lord would judge them and consider David's cause and _____ him from Saul's _____ .
- Saul told David, "You are more _____ than I. You have _____ me _____ , but I have _____ you _____ ."
- Saul then said that David would surely be king, and the kingdom of Israel _____

_____ .

* * * * * *

With these words from King Saul, it would seem that he had repented and no longer would try to kill David. But this did not happen. The evil spirit that had control of Saul would not allow him peace. Saul would not leave David alone.

Finally, when Israel was at war with the Philistines, Saul's sons were killed. The battle was going against Saul's army. Read 1 Samuel 31:4 and explain what finally happened to end his life. _____

_____

_____

_____

_____

_____

An Amalekite told David that Saul was dead. For proof, he showed David Saul's band from his arm and crown. Proudly, the Amalekite claimed that he had killed the king. It would be natural that when David heard about the death of his enemy, Saul, he would be relieved. No longer would he have to run for his life and live in caves and with hardship. But David's heart had never become revengeful. He had never allowed hatred to take control. Read 2 Samuel 1:1-16 and circle the ways in which David showed his feelings at the news of Saul's death.

* * * * * *

- Shouted for joy

- Tore his clothes

- Praised the Amalekite for doing his duty

- Proclaimed a day of celebration

- Mourned and fasted

- Had the Amalekite killed for murdering King Saul

Who Am I?

Read the following Scriptures to determine the correct words to complete the sentences describing a particular Bible character. Then unscramble the circled words to find out who this Bible character is.

- I brought the ____ ____ ◯ to the "City of David" in Jerusalem (2 Samuel 6:12).
- I appointed my son ____ ____ ____ ____ ____ ____ ◯ as my successor (1 Kings 1:32-35).
- ____ __◯__ ____ I avoided Saul's presence and his spear (1 Samuel 18:11).
- In __◯__ ____ ____ ____ ____ ____ ____ ____ ____ I had success because the Lord was with me (1 Samuel 18:14).
- I became one in ____ ____ __◯__ ____ ____ ____ with Jonathan (1 Samuel 18:1).
- I played my ____ __◯__ ____ for the king (1 Samuel 16:23).
- I ____ ____ ____ __◯__ over Israel for forty years (1 Kings 2:11).
- I showed faith in God by killing __◯__ ____ ____ ____ ____ ____ ____ (1 Samuel 17:4, 50).
- The ____ ____ ____ __◯__ called me a man after His own heart (1 Samuel 13:14).

Who Am I? ____ ____ ____ ____   ____ ____ ____ ____ ____

Conquering The Enemy

In the chart below, review the character of David and Saul and then think about your own character. Remember, both David and Saul had a good appearance. They were handsome men. But that was not the most important part of who they were. It was the kind of person they were on the inside that really counted. God wanted to develop godly character in each of these great leaders. Saul chose his own way—the way of self. But David allowed God to develop strength of courage and many other qualities in his life. These are the same qualities God wants to develop in you.

QUALITIES	SAUL	DAVID	YOU
OBEDIENCE/ DISOBEDIENCE			
HATRED/ LOVE			
SELF-CONTROL			
HUMILITY			

21
GOD MOLDS A KING

David's Positions In Life

David was a great man of God and was used of God in so many ways. At various times in his life he was...
• A shepherd boy
• A court musician
• A soldier
• A true friend
• An outcast captain
• A king
• A great general
• A loving father

• A poet
• A sinner
• A brokenhearted man

Read the following verses and decide which item from the list above fits the situation described.

1 Samuel 16:14-23 _____

1 Samuel 17:34-36 _____

1 Samuel 18:1-4 _____

1 Samuel 18:6-7 _____

1 Samuel 18:12-13; 22:1-2 _____

_____

2 Samuel 5:3 _____

2 Samuel 8 and 10 _____

2 Samuel 11 and 12 _____

2 Samuel 18:33 _____

Psalm 8 _____

Psalm 51 _____

David's Strong Character

David had strong Christian character. In fact, God called David "a man after His own heart." Why do you think God thought of David in this way? _____

_____

_____

Write the definitions of each of the following character qualities.

Faithfulness _____

_____

Modesty _____

_____

Patience _____

_____

Courage _____

_____

Forgiving Spirit _____

_____

Penitence _____

_____

Loyalty _____

_____

In the statements below, which of the above traits is being demonstrated in David's life?

► After Saul's death, David did not try to become king of Israel. He waited seven more years; but David knew it was God's plan he should be king of Israel, and he was willing to wait. _____

► Even though Saul hated him and tried to kill him many times, David loved Saul and was sad when he died. _____

► After David sinned against God, he turned to God and repented of his sin.

_____

► David killed lions, bears and a giant.

_____

► David knew God could take care of all his problems. _____

► Even when he knew he would one day be king, David was happy to play the harp and sing for King Saul. _____

98

▶ David would not hurt Saul because Saul was God's anointed one. _____

▶ David trusted God with all his heart. _____

How God Shapes A Man

Michelangelo, a great artist, before beginning a piece of sculpture, said of a piece of marble, "I see an angel in that marble, and I must get him out."

In just as real a way, God was shaping a man out of David. God saw a king in a shepherd lad. This teaches us the lesson that when God looks at us, He sees us, not so much for what we are, but for what we can become as we surrender to Him.

Complete the following sentences by unscrambling the word beneath each line.

* * * * * *

David's start was _____ and discouraging. But David had
                lows

_____ in God. He was _____ and was willing
   hafit   tieanpt

to wait for God to _____. He was _____ before God
              elad   mbeluh

and _____. He gave _____ part of his life to God.
   anm   vreye

David never doubted that God was _____. When he
                      psreume

_____, he was _____ and
   dnnise   ntarpeent

_____; and God forgave him. Because of this _____,
   rrfowusol   ittdueat

God made him a _____ and _____ his life.
         scuescs   deeblss

> **LIFE PRINCIPLE:** Just as God worked on David to make him into the right kind of man, God is also working on your inner character.

Conquering The Enemy

God wants you to have success, and He wants to bless your life also. The reason David became such a great king was because he allowed God to develop his character. Are you willing to give God control of your life so that He might teach you the things you need for your life? _____

We have discussed many areas of inner character in this lesson. What areas do you think God is working on in your life right now? _____

_____

_____

_____

Do you think God has a definite purpose for you? _____ How are you going to find out what God's purpose for you is? _____

_____

_____

_____

_____

_____

22 THE REIGN OF SOLOMON

Reputation And Character

Define reputation. _____

_____

_____

_____

_____

Define character. _____

_____

_____

_____

_____

_____

• Which one is the first part that others see? _____

• Which is the real, genuine you? _____

• Which will eventually be seen by everyone? _____

• Which is more important to God? _____

LIFE PRINCIPLE: If your inner character is right, you will also have a good reputation before others. Your character will eventually show who you really are.

Describe the reputation and character of the following men with one word. Think of the general pattern of their lives.

BIBLE CHARACTER	REPUTATION	CHARACTER
Abraham		
Jacob		
Joseph		
Moses		
Saul		
David		

Solomon: Israel's Third King

Saul and David were opposites when it came to inner character. In the beginning, Saul's reputation was admirable. The people of Israel loved him. But later, when his inner attitudes came out, we see that his reputation was no longer respected.

David was not a perfect man; but even when he sinned before the Lord, his inner character caused him to repent and seek forgiveness. His inner character and his outer reputation were therefore the same. He was a genuine person who did not try to act in a way that was different from the way he felt inside. That is why God called David a "man after His own heart."

When the death of David was near, he called his son, Solomon, into his presence for his final instructions. In 1 Kings 2:2-3, he told Solomon, "_____

_____

_____

_____

_____

_____

_____."

There is no better advice a father can give his son.

Read 1 Kings 3 to learn what made Solomon such a great man and a great king.

_____ If Solomon walked in God's statutes and sacrificed burnt offerings, write a W. If he had others make offerings in his stead, write an O.

_____ If Solomon asked for riches, write an R. If he asked for a discerning heart, write an I.

_____ If God gave Solomon his wish only, write a W. If He gave him riches and honor also, write an S.

_____ If the two women came to Solomon about an argument over a child, write a D. If they argued over money, write an M.

_____ If the real mother wanted the child killed, write a C. If she offered to give the child to the other mother so he could live, write an O.

_____ If all of Israel saw that the wisdom of God was in Solomon, write an M. If they disagreed with his judgments, write a D.

What word did the letters spell?

_____

Now read Proverbs 16:16 to see how important this is. Solomon, who wrote much of the Book of Proverbs, said, " _____

_____

_____

_____

_____

_____."

God had generously answered Solomon's request for wisdom. Throughout the Book of Proverbs, wisdom is shown to be of high attainment; for it shows us how to apply the knowledge of God to our daily lives. Solomon even today is known as the wisest man who ever lived. This gift of God was beyond even Solomon's expectations.

How would you describe Solomon's reputation and character? (See 1 Kings 1:40 and 3:28) _____

_____

_____

_____

_____

The Building Of The Temple

The highlight of Solomon's reign was the building of the temple. God had told David years before that Solomon would be respon-sible for building the temple. Solomon wanted the temple to be so beautiful that it would remind the Israelites of God's greatness, holiness and power. It was to be grander than any other building on earth. The best of materials and the most skilled workmen were used to build the temple.

Read the verses indicated in 1 Kings to be able to provide short answers to the following questions.

* * * * * *

► Did Israel have any adversaries at this time? (5:4) _____

► What type of wood was chosen? (5:10) _____

► Whom did Solomon put in charge? (5:14) _____

► The temple measured _____ long, _____ wide and _____ high (6:2).

► The temple was started in the _____ year after the Israelites left Egypt and in the _____ year of Solomon's reign (6:1).

► The stones were made ready before they were put in the building, so that no _____, _____ or any _____ tool was heard while it was being built (6:7).

► It took _____ years to build the temple (6:37-38).

► What was given a special place in the temple? (8:21) _____

_____

_____

_____

The greatest undertaking of Solomon's reign was the building of the temple. The temple was truly a great monument to God. One stone alone was over thirty-eight feet long. Everything was covered with gold. No other building had such splendor.

When the temple was completed, all of Israel came to Jerusalem to help dedicate the temple to the Lord. Finely crafted furniture and vessels of the finest metals were brought in and put in place. Sacrifices were offered; and Solomon himself knelt before the altar, praising God for His goodness to His people. There was a great celebration that lasted fourteen days.

God's Covenant With Solomon

Then God appeared to Solomon again. Read about this in 1 Kings 9:3-7. What did God promise if Solomon did all He commanded and observed His decrees and laws?

_____

_____

What did He say would happen if Solomon or his sons began to serve other gods and worship them? _____

_____

Complete the following by unscrambling the word beneath each line.

By this time Solomon was indeed a great man. He had a high _____,

tionpiso

great _____, great _____ and many

diswom   thleaw

_____. God had kept His _____ and had

ervsanst   risepoms

overwhelmingly _____ him.

esedbls

* * * * * *

But a change began to come in the heart of Solomon. Being the wisest man did not mean that Solomon always exercised good self-control. Solomon did not always follow his own teachings. Describe what changes began to be evident in the life of Solomon. (11:3-10) _____

_____

_____

_____

_____

_____

Why did God say He would tear part of the kingdom away from Solomon's son? (11:11-13)_____

_____

_____

_____

Should this have been a surprise to Solomon? _____
Why or why not? _____

_____

_____

Look at the time line at the beginning of your book, and you will see that Israel was indeed divided after the death of Solomon.

Conquering The Enemy

God wants to bless your life, but He wants you to surrender to Him. The real temple of God is your body, for the Holy Spirit lives in you. God is more interested in you than in buildings of gold. In the beginning, Solomon glorified God in all he did. The temple was an outward display of the spiritual attitude of Solomon toward God. According to 1 Corinthians 6:19-20, why should you honor God with your body?

_____

_____

_____

_____

_____

Learn a lesson from Solomon's life. Even if you begin by serving the Lord, God can only bless you as long as you continue to serve Him. It is important to continually recommit your life as you grow up to serving the one true God and never turn away from Him. Then, even if you have tribulation from time to time, God will take care of you and bless your life.

23
ELIJAH AND ELISHA

The Divided Kingdom

It is interesting to note that the first three kings of Israel each reigned for forty years. After Solomon's reign, you can see by the Old Testament Time Line that the nation of Israel was divided into two kingdoms. This was a fulfillment of God's covenant with Solomon because he went after other gods. The two kingdoms were Israel and Judah.

The Kingdom Of Israel. This was the northern kingdom. It had ten of the tribes of Israel. The people worshiped idols. This kingdom lasted 209 years and finally fell into the hands of the Assyrians. During that time, there were twenty kings—all of them evil and ungodly. Two of the better known kings were Jeroboam and Ahab. Ahab was the most evil king in the Bible.

The Kingdom Of Judah. This was the southern kingdom. It was comprised of two of the tribes of Israel. There was still worship in the temple of Jerusalem during the 345 years that this kingdom lasted. Judah had nineteen kings and one queen. There were both good and bad kings. The best known included Rehoboam, Jehoshaphat, Joash and Josiah, who found the Word of God after it was lost during the reigns of his father and grandfather. Babylon took this kingdom into captivity.

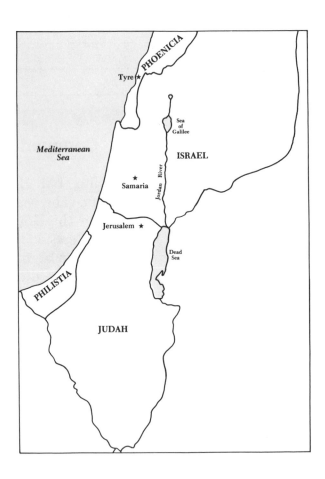

VOCABULARY

Prophet: one who speaks for God and proclaims the Word of God with forcefulness

Two Great Prophets

Now the people had become very sinful. We have seen that for the next 300-400 years following Solomon's death, there were very few godly leaders. So it was that God sent other leaders to speak out for Him.

God will always provide a spokesman for His Word. The two main leaders He sent were prophets: Elijah and Elisha. Let's first compare the personalities of these two men.

ELIJAH	ELISHA
• Great courage • Severe authority • Enthusiastic • Miracles of power	• Great kindness • Very merciful • Love and tenderness • Miracles of kindness

God used both of these men to bring His Word to His people, though they were completely different types of men. God wants to use each of us in a special way too with the abilities He has given each of us.

On the chart below, write the miracles of power that God performed through Elijah.

VERSES	GOD'S POWER SHOWN THROUGH ELIJAH
1 Kings 17:1	
1 Kings 17:17-23	
2 Kings 1:10-12	
2 Kings 2:11-12	

Note: Who watched Elijah go to heaven according to 2 Kings 2:12? _____
What are some of the miracles of kindness that God performed through Elisha?

VERSES	GOD'S LOVE SHOWN THROUGH ELISHA
2 Kings 2:19-22	
2 Kings 4:1-7	
2 Kings 4:32-37	
2 Kings 5:6-14	

There were many other miracles that were performed similarly by both prophets. There were instances when Elijah did miracles of kindness and when Elisha showed the power of God. But in both cases, God used these men to draw His people to repentance.

There were also other differences between the two men. Elijah struggled many times with periods of depression. Explain about one of these times from 1 Kings 19:1-4. _____

_____

_____

_____

_____

Elisha always lived in a spirit of victory. There is no record that he ever got discouraged or depressed. Perhaps the reason for this is the special request he made when Elijah went to be with the Lord. Explain what happened from reading 2 Kings 2:9-12. _____

_____

_____

_____

Conquering The Enemy

What would happen if the sun were gone from the sky? There would be no grass or flowers or orchards—only darkness. We don't often consider what it would be like without different aspects of creation because we know they will always be there. But God is the Creator of all we have. What would it be like if God were gone from all of life? _____

_____

_____

_____

When a leader forgets about the Lord, it is especially serious. A leader such as Solomon has a great responsibility to guide the people in the right way. When the leader is wrong, everything else eventually goes wrong. This is what happened to Israel.

Think about the leaders in your own life. Why is it important for your parents to be the right kind of leaders? _____

_____

_____

_____

_____

Why is it important for your teacher and pastor to be the right kind of leaders?

_____

_____

_____

_____

How can parents and teachers make sure they are the right kind of leaders?

_____

_____

_____

_____

24 EZRA THE TEACHER

Very little is known of what happened in the kingdom of Judah after the destruction of the city of Jerusalem. Babylon left the land devastated. All the major cities were destroyed and not rebuilt for many years. The Israelites now became a part of Babylon. There they built towns and entered into business. Some became wealthy. Many married heathens and forgot about their Jewish heritage. Others were very strong in their religious life.

Rebuilding The Temple

Then Babylon itself fell to Cyrus the Persian. Cyrus had a policy of acknowledging the gods of other countries. He thus decreed that the Jews should return to their homeland. Read Ezra 1 to find out what caused Cyrus to send the Jews back to Jerusalem and what task they were to perform.

_____

_____

VOCABULARY

Heathen: one who does not believe in God or Christianity; pagan

---

_____

_____

Approximately 50,000 Jews returned to Israel. The rest stayed in Babylon. Read the following verses in the Book of Ezra and answer the questions about the events that took place during the next twenty-five years.

► What was the first and most important task? (3:1-6) _____

_____

► What portion of the temple was completed? (3:8-13) _____

► What was the desire of their adversaries? (4:1-2) _____

► What did the enemies do to cause the Jews to stop working? (4:4-5) _____

_____

► List the prophets that God used to again arouse the people to the task (5:1).

► What was the final result? (6:14-16)

_____

The People Return To Jerusalem

Fill in the blanks to complete the following statements.

Ezra 7: Ezra was a descendant from the priestly lineage of _____ (verse 5). His occupation was that of a _____ (verse 11). King _____ stated that all who wanted to go with Ezra to _____ would be allowed to go (verses 11-13). The people were to take _____ and _____ so they could purchase offerings to _____ to God when they arrived in Jerusalem (verses 15-17). Other items needed for the _____ would be provided from the royal _____ (verse 20). Ezra believed that the hand of _____ was upon him and would give him everything he needed (verses 27-28).

Ezra 8: After many days of travel, Ezra discovered that there were no _____ there (verse 15) and therefore no _____ for God's house (verse 17). The people prayed that God would keep them safe, and Ezra refused to take _____ and _____ along to protect the people because he trusted God to protect them (verse 22). After arriving in Jerusalem, the sacred articles were accounted for by _____ and _____ (verses 29-30). The people sacrificed _____ (verse 35) to God and delivered the king's orders to the _____, who gave assistance to the people (verse 36).

Ezra 9: The people had committed the grievous sin of _____

_____

_____ (verses 1-2).

Ezra 10: They showed great repentance by _____

_____

_____ (verse 3).

Ezra's Character Qualities

We have already seen that Ezra's life was one that showed great strength of character. The traits that we can learn the most from Ezra's example are...
- Faith
- Self-denial
- Trustworthiness
- Man of prayer
- Studied God's Word
- Taught God's Word to others

Read the following verses. Then state what Ezra is doing in each and the character quality that is seen in his life.

EZRA	SITUATION	QUALITY
7:10		
7:11		
7:13-26		
8:21; 10:1		
8:22		
10:6		

Conquering The Enemy

God was very upset that the Israelites had intermarried with heathen or ungodly people. We must remember that Christ calls us out to be a special, unique and separated people. He cannot work His plan and give the blessings He desires to give to those who are a part of Satan's kingdom. Read 2 Corinthians 6:14-17. List as many phrases as you can that teach this principle.

_____

_____

_____

_____

_____

In what areas of your own life do you think God would have you follow this principle? Think about such areas in your life as your friends, movies you see, television programs you watch, music you listen to, etc.

_____

_____

_____

_____

Now read 2 Corinthians 6:18. What is God's promise to you if you obey Him by separating yourself from unrighteousness?

_____

_____

25
NEHEMIAH—THE GREAT ORGANIZER

We have seen how God created a desire in the heart of a heathen king to rebuild the temple to the living God in Jerusalem. The Jews had left Babylon and rebuilt the temple in Jerusalem. The temple was completed in 516 B.C. Almost sixty years later, Ezra arrived in Jerusalem with another group of Jews. He had looked forward to worshiping the Lord in the temple but was disappointed to see God's people living in sin. Ezra's task was to turn the Jews in Jerusalem back to God.

Now thirteen years had passed, and a man named Nehemiah learned that the walls of Jerusalem were still in ruins. Nehemiah lived in Persia during the reign of King Artaxerxes and was cupbearer to the king. This was a very important position. But Nehemiah now asked the king for permission to return to Jerusalem to rebuild the walls of the city. This lesson teaches how Nehemiah accomplished this great task by organizing the people of God.

Nehemiah's Mission

► What did Nehemiah learn concerning Jerusalem? (1:3) _____

_____

► What was his immediate reaction? (1:4-11) _____

_____

VOCABULARY

Usury: charging high interest rates for loans to the poor

► Who was the king? What difference did the king see in Nehemiah? What was Nehemiah's request? Did the king grant his request? (2:1-6) _____

_____

_____

_____

_____

► What did Nehemiah do first when he arrived in Jerusalem? What do you think his purpose was in doing this? (2:11-16) _____

_____

_____

► What goal did Nehemiah set? What was the attitude of the other men who were with him? (2:17-18) _____

_____

_____

_____

Nehemiah's Organizational Plan

Read Nehemiah chapter 3. Explain the general plan of organization that was used to complete the walls around the city. Do not discuss the plan in detail by naming each section.

_____

_____

_____

_____

_____

Facing Opposition

Many times when we are trying to do what is right, others try to discourage and defeat us. This is one of the ways Satan tries to affect our lives. We must learn to recognize when Satan is trying to gain control and not allow him to defeat us.

In the case of the Israelites who were working to rebuild the walls of Jerusalem under the direction of Nehemiah, the opposition came in many forms. Read the verses listed in the chart on the next page. Then decide whether the opposition came through selfish greed, anger, ridicule, discouragement or plotting. Finally, explain how the builders overcame the opposition.

NEHEMIAH	TYPE OF OPPOSITION	HOW OPPOSITION WAS OVERCOME
2:19-20		
4:3-6		
4:7-9		
4:10-14		
5:1-17		

Now read Nehemiah 6:15-16. What was the final outcome in these verses, and what effect did it have on those who gave such strong opposition? _____

_____

_____

How many days did it take to build the walls? _____

Lessons On Leadership

Nehemiah is one of the great leaders of the Bible. His leadership is not evidenced by great speaking ability but in his ability to organize people to do great projects. The rebuilding of the walls around Jerusalem was a monumental task that required great leadership skills.

To be a good leader, you need to learn qualities of leadership. Read the following verses and use them as a basis to make a list of lessons you need to learn in order to become a good leader.

* * * * * *

Exodus 18:21— _____

_____

Deuteronomy 1:17— _____

_____

Joshua 1:7— _____

_____

Joshua 1:12-15— _____

_____

1 Samuel 12:23— _____

Mark 10:44-45— _____

Conquering The Enemy

Think about each of the types of opposition faced by the Israelites as they built the walls of Jerusalem. Can you think of a time when you faced these types of opposition from others? Write an example for each of the following from your own experiences.

* * * * * *

Greed of others _____

_____

Anger _____

_____

Ridicule _____

_____

Discouragement _____

_____

Plotting _____

_____

26 QUEEN ESTHER

Suppose we as a nation had to depend on just one person to save us all from being killed. That is exactly what happened in Old Testament times. And it was not a man God used, but a woman.

As we study this story, notice God's hand in every detail. Chapters 1 and 2 tell the story of how Esther was made queen. Her husband's kingdom, Persia, covered half the known world. He was very powerful. All of the verses you will use to complete the story below are from the Book of Esther.

* * * * * *

► Esther was a Jewish girl who was adopted and raised by her cousin, _____ (2:7).

► God allowed Mordecai to _____ (2:21-23).

► A man named _____ was given the highest position next to the king (3:1).

► The people were commanded to _____

_____ (3:2).

► Haman was angry at Mordecai because _____

_____ (3:5).

► Why wouldn't Mordecai do as Haman wished? _____

_____

_____

► What great sin does this tell you was in Haman's heart? _____

► This was really such a little offense, wasn't it? But Haman's heart was so full of pride and so evil that Mordecai became the biggest problem in his life. Haman was so wicked that he decided to kill Mordecai, but not just him alone. He wanted the king to _____

_____

_____

_____ (3:6).

VOCABULARY
Fasting: to abstain from food or drink for a set period of time for a holy or religious purpose

► Did the king agree to this? (3:10-11) _____

► When Esther heard this, she was " _____ " (4:4).

► Mordecai wanted Esther to _____

_____ (4:8).

► Esther was afraid to go to her husband because of a law which said _____

_____ (4:10-11).

► Mordecai told Esther, "And who knows but that you have come to royal position for such a time as this?" (4:14). What did Mordecai mean by this? _____

_____

_____

► What was Esther's attitude now? (4:16) _____

_____

► How do you know God had prepared the king's heart before Esther came? (5:1-3)

_____

_____

_____

► Esther invited the king and Haman to a banquet. Haman was filled with even more _____ (5:11-12).

► Haman planned now to _____

_____ (5:14).

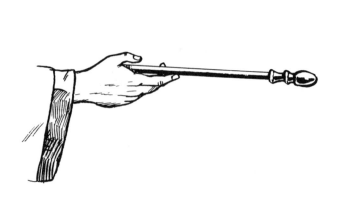

▶ That night the Lord reminded the king that _____

_____

_____ (6:1-3).

▶ Read 6:4-11. Who thought he was going to be honored and exalted? _____
Whom did the king intend to have honored? _____

Why? _____

▶ Esther told the king about the plot to kill her people. The king's wrath was extreme.
Whom did he have hanged on the gallows prepared for Mordecai? (7:9-10) _____
The king then found a way to save the Jewish nation from being destroyed. Then Mordecai

_____

_____

_____ (10:3).

```
┌─────────────────────────────────────────────────────────────────────────────┐
│                                                                               │
│   LIFE PRINCIPLE: Man's happenings are God's plans.                           │
│                                                                               │
└─────────────────────────────────────────────────────────────────────────────┘
```

Who is really in control of all things? _____
If this is truly so, then...

★ Why was Esther in the right place at the right time? _____

_____

★ Why had God allowed Mordecai to save the king's life? _____

_____

★ Why did the king allow the Jews to live? _____

_____

Conquering The Enemy

Esther was successful for God because she trusted in Him and had the courage to do what God wanted her to do. What might have happened if Esther had been afraid to go before the king? _____

_____

_____

_____

_____

Describe a situation in which you had to have the courage to do something that was very difficult for you to do, but you knew it was the right thing to do. _____

_____

_____

_____

_____

27
WHY GOD ALLOWS TRIALS

We have been learning about the importance of our personal character and about surrendering our lives to the control of the Holy Spirit and standing for what is right even if we stand alone.

Now we must learn more about the work of Satan because even though we are Christians, Satan wants us to be unhappy in our lives and not have faith in God. Sometimes we blame things on Satan that are really our own fault. But there are also times when God allows Satan to test us in order that our character might be strengthened. During such times, we must remember that Satan cannot test a Christian unless God allows him to. God is still the divine controller of our lives. This is what we learn from the story of Job.

As we start our lesson, first think about a time at which it would have been easy to blame some sin on Satan, but it was really

your own fault. _____
_____
_____
_____
_____
_____
_____
_____
_____

It is most important that we learn to take responsibility for our own actions and confess our sins to God when we are guilty of some wrongdoing. But we must also realize that even when we do our best and live wisely, sometimes we have periods of "trials" or "testing." This is what happened to a man named Job.

What Job Was Like

The story of Job most likely took place during the time of Abraham. The Book of Job therefore chronologically fits during the time of the Book of Genesis.

Read the first chapter of the Book of Job and answer the following questions.

Where did Job live? _____

_____

How many sons did he have? _____
How many daughters? _____
How many sheep? _____ Camels? _____
Oxen? _____
What kind of man was Job? _____

_____

_____

_____

_____

_____

The key verse in understanding the character of Job is found in 1:22, which states, " _____

_____

_____

_____

_____

_____ ."

Satan's Charge Against Job

What was Satan's charge against Job? (1:10-11) _____

_____

_____

_____

To whom was the charge made? _____

This is exactly how Satan works against us. Satan is always ready to accuse us and attack us whenever he thinks he can find a weakness. How is he described in 1 Peter 5:8? _____

_____

_____

As Christians, we can be sure that God will not allow Satan to tempt us unless He has a definite purpose. Satan was telling God that Job and other Christians only serve Him because of all His blessings. God wanted to show Satan that Job would have faith even if everything were taken away. Job was a very wealthy man. What did God allow Satan to do? (1:12-22) _____

_____

_____

_____

_____

Job's Faith In God

God had allowed Satan to take away all Job's riches and possessions. But Satan was still not satisfied. What did he say to God now? (2:5) _____

_____

God gave Satan permission to do anything except _____ (2:6).

What happened to Job next? (2:7-8) _____

Did Job lose faith in God? (2:10) _____

* * * * * *

Job did not understand all that God had allowed to happen. Many times we say, "If God loves me like He says He does, why do these things happen to me?" God wants us to learn to have faith in Him, as we see in the example of Job. We do not always immediately understand God's purposes, for "His ways are higher than our ways."

Job's Friends

Job's friends came and tried to comfort him. They suggested that he must find out the cause of his problems. They felt that he was probably being punished for sin and must therefore repent of the sin.

His friend, Eliphaz, said, "Do not despise

_____

_____" (5:17).

Bildad comforted Job with the words, "God does not _____

_____

_____" (8:20).

Many times this is true. God does discipline us when He wants us to repent of

some sin in our lives. But there are also times when we have done no wrong, and testing still comes. Job insisted that he had not sinned, and therefore his misfortunes were not the result of his sins. Job did have faith in God. Even though he did not understand what God was doing, he trusted Him.

In your own words, explain Job's feelings toward the Lord at the end of the story (42:1-3). _____

_____

_____

_____

God's Purpose In Trials

In the story of Job, we have seen how God allows His children to go through trials in order to make us become more and more like Jesus Christ. See Romans 8:28 and 29. When you might tend at times to feel sorry for yourself, think instead of the One who

suffered for all of our sins. Who suffered all things for us? _____

Think about an athlete preparing for a big race. To be a great athlete takes much strict discipline and hard training and practice. Christ is ever preparing us for the race that is set before us. See Hebrews 12:1. He wants us to throw off our _____ and run with _____ in the race.

The Final Chapter

Read Job 42:10-17. Job's friends had left him. How did Job respond to this? _____
_____

Do you think Job still had faith in God? _____

Describe the blessings given to Job. Compare the prosperity of Job at the end of the story with what he had in the beginning. _____
_____
_____

Conquering The Enemy

There is a reason and a purpose for everything God allows to happen in our lives. Copy Romans 8:28 to see how God Himself explains this fact. _____
_____
_____
_____

Name at least one thing in your life right now that you must trust God for, even though you don't understand all the circumstances. _____
_____
_____

Remember: Most of our problems are not caused by Satan. They are caused by _____ .

28 SONGS OF PRAISE TO GOD

All of us face disappointments and hurts from time to time in our lives. God is aware of how we feel during such times, and that is one reason He prepared the Book of Psalms for us. Most of the psalms were written to help us to get over our hurts and frustrated feelings. They also put our minds on the Lord Jesus who will help our hurts to be healed. Then we can again praise God fully because we know it is He who has helped us.

Learning To Praise God

What does the word "psalm" mean?

_____

_____

_____

_____

VOCABULARY

Blessed: having or receiving divine favor that produces inner peace and joy
Meditate (meditation): to think deeply and continually about something
Psalm: a sacred song or poem

The Book of Psalms is a book of praise to God. It contains 150 poems to be set to music for worship. They are songs to be learned and sung and applied to our hearts. Through the Psalms we see our lives pictured in every experience of joy, sorrow, victory and failure. David is the principal author of the Psalms, but there are other authors also. Notice whose names are given as authors of the following.

- Psalms 50, 73-83— _____
- Psalm 88— _____
- Psalm 89— _____
- Psalm 90— _____

Praising God in all things and developing a grateful spirit for all His goodness to us is the highest calling we have, for "man's chief end is to glorify God."

As you begin to learn the beauty and worth of the Psalms to express your own feelings and attitudes, you will want to make them a part of your very life. In this lesson you will learn how this can be done and the value it can have for your own life.

"Blessed Is The Man..."

Look at Psalm 1. What word begins the Book of Psalms? _____

What is the definition of this word?

_____

_____

_____

This word is used again and again in this book, for this is what God wants to do for your life. Read the verses listed in the chart below. From each verse, tell whom God will bless and why He blesses them.

PSALM	WHOM GOD BLESSES	WHY HE BLESSES THEM
1:1-2		
2:12		
33:12		
84:5		
94:12		
119:2		

Learning About Jesus Christ

Many of the verses of the Psalms refer to Jesus Christ. Read the following verses and find the word or phrases that refer to our Savior.

2:2 _____

16:10 _____

22:16 and 18 _____

_____

34:20 _____

_____

115:11 _____

118:22 _____

Meditation In The Word

In your own words, explain why the Lord wants you to memorize Scripture.

_____

_____

Memorization of God's Word is very important, but there is an even more important activity that we must learn about. What is the meaning of the word "meditate"? _____

_____

_____

Meditation is one activity that God promises to bless by giving us success in life.

Read Psalm 1:2-3 and see how God expresses the need for meditation.

► On what are we to meditate? _____
► When should we meditate? _____
► What will be the result? _____

_____

Now read Psalm 119:97-100 and find out more promises for meditation.

► How often are we to meditate? _____
► List at least three results of meditation.

✔ _____
✔ _____
✔ _____

Now read Joshua 1:8 to further understand the importance of meditation.

► What are we to do with God's Word? _____
► Why are we to do this? _____

_____

► What will be the result? _____

_____

We are to meditate on all of God's Word, but the Psalms are especially good for meditation because their thoughts can easily become a part of our thinking. The Psalms express our feelings and thoughts.

Spiritual Lessons From The Psalms

While the Psalms are primarily songs and poems that are meant to help us with our moods and feelings, many of them give warnings to the wicked and lessons to Christians. Read each of the following verses from the Psalms and explain the lesson taught.

★ How does God respond to the wicked? (2:1-5) _____

_____

_____

★ What place has God given man in the universe? (8:4-5) _____

_____

_____

★ How does God respond to those who trust in their wealth? (49:6-9) _____

_____

_____

★ What are we to do when we have great problems? (61:1-3) _____

_____

_____

★ What does God teach about the home? (127:3-4) _____

_____

_____

LIFE PRINCIPLE: When you memorize Scripture and that is all you do with it, it will become a part of your memory; but this does not always mean that it will become a part of you! When you learn to meditate, you will...
• Fill your mind with God's thoughts and attitudes
• Allow God's Word to change your feelings and attitudes
• Have the understanding and ability to make correct choices for your life so you will be a success

---

Conquering The Enemy

Now explain in your own words why God wants you to do more than just memorize His Word and what He promises to those who make the Word a part of their hearts and lives through meditation. _____

_____

_____

_____

_____

29
KNOWLEDGE, WISDOM AND UNDERSTANDING

The Book of Proverbs teaches moral truths about how to live on earth. Proverbs is a book of wisdom from God. Because it is a book that has the goal to make us wise, most people think Solomon wrote the book. He did write most of it, but there were other authors as well.

Three Areas Of Learning

In His Word God talks about three areas of learning: knowledge, wisdom and understanding. Let's begin by looking at the meanings of these words.

Knowledge is learning basic facts. For example, you know that Columbus discovered America in 1492, and you also know that George Washington was the first President of the United States.

Wisdom is learning to apply these facts or ideas to your own life. For example, you may know that stealing is wrong; but wisdom is deciding that you will never steal. A person who steals from another is not wise.

Understanding is seeing things from God's point of view. God has reasons for His commands, and we must understand His purposes. Stealing, for example, is harmful to others. God wants everyone's rights protected. God does not want you to steal nor does He want others to steal from you. Learn to understand God's point of view.

The Bible says, "The fear of the Lord is the beginning of knowledge." Many people who are not Christians have a great deal of knowledge; but only a Christian can have true wisdom and understanding, for these come only from God. Copy Proverbs 2:6 to see that these come only from God.

_____

_____

_____

_____

_____

VOCABULARY

Fool: someone who is not interested in good instruction; someone who does not fear God

Knowledge: learning facts

Wisdom: learning to apply facts to your own life; good judgment

Understanding: seeing things from God's point of view

God Commands...God Promises

To have wisdom, we must first obey God's instructions. As we obey God, we learn that we can trust Him to keep promises. We also learn that God never gives a command without the promise of a blessing if we obey. To see an example of this, study Proverbs 3:1-10. First write the commandment and then the promise. The first one has been done for you.

GOD'S COMMAND	GOD'S PROMISE FOR OBEDIENCE
3:1—Keep God's commands	3:2—Long life, prosperity
3:3—	3:4—
3:5-6—	3:6—
3:7—	3:8—
3:9—	3:10—

Listen To Instruction

It is God's plan that we all have people over us to teach us and instruct us in the ways of God. Read the following verses in the Book of Proverbs to see those by whom God wants you to be instructed.

4:1 _____

6:20 _____

8:1, 10 _____

Practical Lessons For Life

The most interesting and important part of the teachings of Proverbs is the practical lessons on everyday problems that are taught in its pages. Use a concordance and find a verse that gives a teaching of God for each of the following areas. You will write down only one verse; but you will see that there are many, many things that God wants us to know about each subject.

* * * * * *

■ Friends _____

_____

_____

■ Idleness (laziness, being a sluggard) _____

_____

_____

■ Lying (speaking what is false) _____

_____

_____

■ Conduct _____

_____

_____

■ Gossip _____

_____

_____

■ Boasting _____

_____

_____

The Book Of Ecclesiastes

Most of the people in the world live their lives never considering God's will for their lives. Even Christians often do not consider how God wants to work in their lives. The Book of Ecclesiastes discusses the lack of understanding of such people.

There are two phrases used throughout this book. The first phrase is "under the sun." This expression is used 29 times. What do you think it refers to? _____

_____

The second phrase describes the best that we can have apart from God. Most men, like the writer, try to find happiness and a life of meaning. But apart from God, they find that "everything is meaningless." What does this phrase mean? _____

_____

Now read and discuss Ecclesiastes 2:11, 16-18; 8:15-17. Then tell in your own words what conclusion the writer came to after living life for himself. _____

_____

_____

Ideas From Ecclesiastes

Read the following verses in the Book of Ecclesiastes to complete the puzzle and learn more about the main ideas in the book.

3:1—There is a time and a (8 across) for everything.
3:11—"He has made everything (5 across) in its time."
4:9—"Two are better than one, because they have a good (1 down) for their (7 down)."
4:12—"Though one may be overpowered, two can (4 down) themselves."
4:13—It is better to be a "poor but (6 across) youth" than a (2 down) king.
5:3—A (10 across) comes with many (11 across), and a fool speaks too many (6 down).
8:3—"Do not stand up for a bad (3 across)."
11:9—"Be (9 down), young man, while you are (12 across)."

Conquering The Enemy

List those people in your life whom God is using to instruct you and make you wise. Beside each person you name, tell something specific they have taught you about how to live wisely. _____

_____

_____

_____

_____

_____

No one wants to be thought of as a fool. According to Proverbs 1:7, who is a fool?

_____

_____

_____

Consider those whom God has placed in your life to teach you. Do you really listen to them and follow what they say, or do you tend to do what you want to do anyway? Do you then, according to God's Word, think you are wise; or are you a fool?

_____

30 THREE PROPHETS OF GOD

We have already studied the lives of two great prophets of God: Elijah and Elisha. Remember, the prophet was God's messenger bringing a message from God to man. After the death of Solomon, we also learned that Israel became a divided kingdom. With the rule of so many bad kings who did not care about God's Word, God began to speak through the voices of prophets. Read Isaiah 1:4 and explain in your own words what had happened to the people of Israel. _____

_____

_____

_____

Thus, during this time, God raised up prophets to warn His people and bring them back to Himself.

Isaiah

Isaiah is thought of by many as the greatest prophet in the Word of God. The

> ### VOCABULARY
>
> Desolate: laid waste; uninhabited

story of how God called Isaiah to prophesy in His name is found in Isaiah 6.

► Describe the vision Isaiah saw (6:1-4).

_____

_____

► How did Isaiah see himself before God? (6:5) _____

_____

► What did God do for Isaiah? (6:6-7)

_____

_____

► For whom was God looking? (6:8)

_____

_____

► What was Isaiah's response to God? (6:8)

_____

_____

The people of Judah had been taken captive by Babylon. Babylon was a great and magnificent city. It was rich and powerful. During this time God had Isaiah make a prophecy concerning this city. What was the prophecy? (13:19-22) _____

_____

_____

_____

_____

Today, if you visited Babylon, you would see that the prophecy has indeed come true. Even today, there is only ruin and desolation. No one lives where Babylon, the great city, once existed—only bats and owls make their homes in the ruins.

All through the Book of Isaiah, prophecy is given about future events. Many of them have already come true such as the ruin of Babylon; others are still to happen such as the second coming of Christ. Still many other prophecies concerning Christ have already come true. Isaiah lived 700 years before Christ came to earth. Let us see what the Lord led him to prophesy about Jesus Christ. Read the following verses and tell what they foretold about Jesus' life. Notice that all of them have already come true.

* * * * * *

1:18 _____

_____

7:14 _____

_____

9:6 _____

_____

53:2-12 _____

_____

Jeremiah

Jeremiah was another great prophet of God. As you read about Jeremiah's call from God, notice how personally the Lord talked to Jeremiah. God wants to have a very close relationship with each of us. Read Jeremiah 1 and answer the following.

► When did the Lord first know Jeremiah and plan his life? (1:5) _____

_____

_____

_____

► God has a plan for every person. Most people are afraid to be a part of God's plan. They make excuses. What excuse was made in verse 6? _____

_____

_____

► We must understand that we are part of God's plan, and He will work out the details. We only have to be willing. What was the Lord's answer to Jeremiah's excuse? (1:7) _____

_____

_____

► Many times we are just afraid to do what we should. We may be afraid of what others will think, or perhaps we must give up selfish desires. What is the Lord's answer to this problem? (1:8) _____

_____

_____

_____

► Since Jeremiah was called to be a prophet of God, God made commitments to him.

What promises were made in verses 9 and 10? _____

_____

_____

_____

_____

_____

One of the most important roles of a prophet was to proclaim the truth of God. God wanted to use Jeremiah to tell the people what would happen if they did not turn back to Him. God does not want to punish us or be cruel, but He will warn us of what will happen if we do not listen to Him. Then it is our choice and when problems come because of our disobedience, we cannot blame anyone but ourselves.

What did God tell the people would happen to their land? (26:7-9) _____

_____

_____

What did Jeremiah tell the people they must do so the prophecy would not come true? (26:12-13) _____

_____

_____

The people would not listen to Jeremiah, and God allowed them to be taken captive. But even then, God made them a new promise. What was this promise? (29:10)

_____

_____

_____

Sometimes God must allow hardships to come to bring us closer to Him. Troublesome times are never fun, but they are always for our good. During such times

God's thoughts toward us are never bad. Copy Jeremiah 29:11 to see God's attitude.

_____

_____

_____

_____

_____

_____

Ezekiel

It is important to remember that when we study the prophets and hear their voices through the Scriptures, it is really God Himself who is speaking. The prophets were truly the voice of God to an unbelieving nation.

One phrase occurs 47 times in the Book of Ezekiel. This phrase is important because it teaches us that it truly is God who is speaking and that Ezekiel and the other prophets were instruments of God. Compare the following three verses and write the phrase that appears in each.

* * * * * *

Ezekiel 15:1   Ezekiel 24:15   Ezekiel 33:1

_____

Now see if you can find two more places in Ezekiel where this phrase is used. Write the verse references below.

_____

What do you think this phrase means? _____

_____

Now read 2 Peter 1:21 and copy the verse below. _____

_____

_____

Why is this verse important in showing the trustworthiness of the Scriptures?

_____

_____

To learn more from the Book of Ezekiel, read the following verses to complete the puzzle.

DOWN:
1. The word of the Lord came to Ezekiel during the "fifth year of the exile of _____ _____" (1:2).
3. The Lord said that Israel's foolish prophets were like jackals among _____ (13:4).
4. The appearance of the living creatures Ezekiel saw was like burning _____ of fire (1:13).
5. The _____ of the Lord came upon Ezekiel (11:5).
7. The _____ of the Lord came to Ezekiel (23:1).
9. "You will see things that are even more _____ than this" (8:15).
10. "Above the expanse over their heads was what looked like a throne of _____" (1:26).
11. The men of Israel took bribes to _____ _____ (22:12).

ACROSS:
2. The name of the city in Ezekiel's vision: _____ _____ _____ _____ (48:35).
6. The Lord told Ezekiel to go to the house of _____ (3:4).
8. The feet of the four living creatures "gleamed like _____ _____" (1:7).
10. God will cause the hordes to fall by the _____ of mighty men (32:12).
12. The king of Babylon whom God brought against Tyre (26:7).

31
DANIEL—A COURAGEOUS YOUNG MAN

Probably more than any other man in God's Word, Daniel's life is a testimony of one who had the courage to stand for what is right. Again and again in his story, we see Daniel placed in situations in which he had to choose to stand for right, even if it meant death.

Because Israel had turned against God, they had been taken into captivity. But even though Israel as a nation had turned against God, there were still individuals who stood for God; and God greatly blessed their lives. Daniel was one of these people.

When Daniel was very young, he was taken captive into Babylon. The rest of Daniel's life was spent in the beautiful city of Babylon. From the moment Daniel arrived at the palace, he determined to take a stand for the one true God. Daniel and his companions took part in several moral conflicts, and it is these conflicts that we will study below.

Conflict #1—The King's Diet

Describe Daniel and explain why he had

VOCABULARY
Defile: to corrupt; to make filthy

been brought to the palace (1:3-4).

_____

_____

_____

_____

_____

Now read Daniel 1:5 and 8-16. Outline the events of this conflict below.

THE COMMAND: _____

_____

_____

DANIEL'S COMMITMENT: _____

_____

_____

_____

_____

THE TIME OF PROVING: _____

_____

_____

_____

THE RESULT: _____

_____

_____

We have learned this year that obedience to God brings great blessing in our lives. How did God bless Daniel and his friends' lives, and who particularly took note of this? (1:17-20)

_____

_____

_____

Conflict #2—The King's Dream

Read Daniel 2. Then match the question on the left with the correct answer on the right.

_____ What did King Nebuchadnezzar want the magicians, enchanters, sorcerers and astrologers to do?

_____ What was going to happen to all the wise men if they could not do this?

_____ What excuse did the astrologers make?

_____ How did Daniel respond to hearing the king's decree?

_____ What was Daniel's first response when he learned the interpretation of the dream?

_____ What was Nebuchadnezzar's attitude toward the God of Daniel then?

_____ How did God use King Nebuchadnezzar to reward Daniel?

A. He praised God for His sovereignty.

B. They said no one could answer the king because only gods could tell it, and gods do not live among men.

C. He fell down and honored Him as the God of gods and Lord of kings.

D. He wanted them to tell him the dream he had forgotten and then interpret it for him.

E. Daniel was made ruler over the entire province and placed in charge of all its wise men.

F. They would all be killed.

G. He told the king he would interpret the dream; he then received the interpretation from God in a vision.

Conflict #3—The King's Image

Daniel and his friends had handled themselves very wisely. Now Daniel's three friends would be tested much more severely. King Nebuchadnezzar had acknowledged that Daniel's God was the God of all gods. But he did not worship Him as the only true God. He still worshiped other gods and believed that he as king should also be worshiped. Review the story in Daniel 3.

* * * * * *

► What were the names of Daniel's three friends? _____

_____

► Explain the situation which caused them to show that they had great courage to do right.

_____

_____

_____

► What punishment was given because of the stand they took? _____

_____

► What was Nebuchadnezzar's attitude toward God at first? (3:15) _____

_____

► How did God take care of them through this? _____

_____

_____

► What was Nebuchadnezzar's attitude toward the true God after they had taken their stand and been delivered from being burned while in the furnace? (3:29-30) _____

_____

_____

Conquering The Enemy

Many of the Jews who had been taken into captivity had accepted the loose morals and religion of Babylon. Though others fell away, Daniel and his friends kept themselves apart from the evil of the court where they lived. They were true to God in a day when everything was against them. It was hard to refuse the excellent food of the king. It would have been much easier to have bowed before the idol. But through their obedience, God greatly blessed them.

How do you think your testimony would have held up if you had been in their place?

The following questions may help you understand how much courage you have in your own heart.

* * * * * *

• Do you think standing alone for God is hard? _____ Do you believe it is necessary? _____

• Do you think standing for right is sissy, or do you believe it takes courage?

_____

• Do you have to have the teacher in the room to make sure you are working?

_____

• Can your friends lead you to do things that are wrong in God's eyes? _____

• Do you cheat? _____ Use bad language? _____ Lie? _____ Steal? _____

• Who is most important for you to obey—God or man? _____

32 DANIEL'S CONFLICTS CONTINUE

Conflict #4—The King's Banquet

Belshazzar was the Babylonian ruler who succeeded Nebuchadnezzar as king. One day this king gave a great banquet in honor of his gods. Read Daniel 5 and fill in the blanks to see what happened as a result of this banquet.

* * * * * *

Belshazzar invited _____ nobles to the banquet. The gold and silver goblets used were brought from the _____ in _____ by _____. At the banquet all the nobles praised _____ _____ .

Suddenly all the festivities came to a halt because a _____ was seen writing on the _____. Everyone was very frightened. The king promised that anyone who could read the writing would be clothed in _____, have a _____ placed around his neck and be the third highest _____ in the _____. None of the king's wise men could read the writing.

Then the queen remembered _____. When offered the reward, Daniel said, "_____ _____."

Daniel accused Belshazzar of _____.
The writing said that (1) God had _____ the days of his reign and brought it to an _____; (2) his kingdom had been weighed and found _____ and (3) his kingdom was to be _____ and given to the _____ and _____.

Conflict #5—The King's Decree

Read Daniel 5:30-6:24. Then match the beginnings of the sentences with the correct endings by writing the correct letter.

_____ The new king of Babylon

_____ The king appointed three administrators and 120 satraps

_____ The king planned to set Daniel over all these leaders because of

_____ The administrators and satraps tried to find grounds for charges against Daniel

_____ Finally, the only accusation they could charge him with

_____ In order to trap Daniel, a law was made that stated

_____ Instead of discontinuing his prayers,

_____ The king was upset when he found out but could not change the law

_____ God protected Daniel in the lions' den by

_____ Daniel's accusers

A. His exceptional qualities.

B. But they were unable to do so.

C. For thirty days, everyone should pray to the king.

D. Sending His angel to close the lions' mouths.

E. Because a law signed by the king could not be changed.

F. Had to do with the law of his God.

G. Daniel prayed three times a day where all could see him.

H. Were themselves devoured by the hungry lions.

I. Was Darius.

J. To rule over the kingdom.

The Character Of Daniel

Daniel's life is an example to us of godly character. Read each passage in the following chart, describe the situation found there, and then decide what character quality is being shown in Daniel's life.

DANIEL	SITUATION	CHARACTER SHOWN
1:8		
2:17-18		

DANIEL	SITUATION	CHARACTER SHOWN
5:22-23		
6:4		
6:10		
10:3		

Conquering The Enemy

Daniel and his friends showed great loyalty to God in spite of a very difficult situation. They had been taken away from their parents to another land. Neither their parents nor anyone else from their homeland would ever know if they had kept their commitment to God. They demonstrated loyalty because they truly loved and trusted God. From what we have studied about Daniel and his friends, list some tests that they faced and then proved their loyalty to God by the way they responded.

* * * * * *

■ TEST ONE: _____
_____
_____

■ TEST TWO: _____
_____
_____

■ TEST THREE: _____
_____

Has your loyalty to God, your family or your friends ever been tested? Explain how you were tested and how you responded to the test. _____
_____
_____
_____
_____
_____

33 THE PROPHET WHO RAN

The story of Jonah is often thought to be fantasy or fiction, for it contains some aspects that we would not consider to be natural. The idea that a man could live in the belly of a large fish for three days does not seem possible. As Christians who believe God's Word literally, we know that the story is true because it is part of the Bible. But when we realize that Jesus Himself mentioned the story of Jonah as factual, we know even more certainly that the story of Jonah is true in every detail.

The story of Jonah can be divided into four sections: Jonah's disobedience, God's discipline, God's deliverance and Jonah's decision.

Jonah's Disobedience

Read Jonah 1:1-3 and explain the following. What did God command Jonah to do? What did Jonah do instead? _____

_____

_____

_____

_____

_____

_____

We need to understand more about Jonah's feelings. You see, Nineveh was part of a very powerful, wicked and evil nation. The people of Nineveh had done terrible deeds to the Israelites, and Jonah was bitter against them. Jonah believed they deserved severe punishment. Thus he did not want to warn them of God's judgment; for, if they should repent, God would save them.

God's Discipline

Read Jonah 1:4-17 and fill in the blanks.

Now Jonah was on a ship fleeing from the Lord. But the Lord sent a great _____ so that it seemed the ship was going to _____. The men on the ship were _____ and began to cry out to their _____. They began to throw contents of the ship into the sea. Jonah, meanwhile, was _____. The ship's captain asked Jonah to call _____ so they would not perish. Then all the men cast _____ to find out who was responsible for the storm, and the lot fell on _____.

Now, when the men asked Jonah what he had done, Jonah explained that _____

_____

_____

_____ (1:10).
When the men asked Jonah what should be done to calm the sea, Jonah told them they should _____
_____. The men tried to row and to bring the boat to shore, but the sea became even wilder. Finally, they took Jonah and _____
_____ ;
and the sea _____.
Now the Lord had provided a _____
_____ to _____

Jonah. And Jonah was inside the fish _____ days and _____ nights.

From what you have read in this part of the story, how do you know that Jonah had a good heart and was courageous? _____

_____

_____

_____

_____

_____

_____

God's Deliverance

Read Jonah 2 and explain what Jonah did while he was in the belly of the fish.

_____

_____

How did God respond? _____

_____

Jonah's Decision

Now read Jonah 3. Had God changed His mind about what He wanted Jonah to do? _____ How did Jonah respond this time? _____

_____

What was the message that Jonah proclaimed when he arrived in Nineveh?

_____

_____

What did the people of Nineveh do immediately? _____

_____

_____

When God saw their works, that they turned from their evil ways, He _____

_____

_____ .

A Picture Of Christ

Before we finish studying the story of Jonah, let's realize that Jonah is a picture of Jesus Christ. See how many similarities between Jonah and Christ you can think of. Matthew 12:40 will help you. _____

_____

_____

_____

_____

The story also shows us the character of God. What does God's concern for the people of Nineveh teach us about Him? _____

_____

_____

Conquering The Enemy

From reading Jonah 4:1, had Jonah changed his attitude about the people of Nineveh? _____ Jonah knew the attitude of God towards all people, for in verse 2 he described God as "_____

_____

_____ ."

If Jonah had been able to see the problem from God's point of view, he could have had compassion and love for even the sinful people of Nineveh. All of us, however, know how difficult it is to see everything from God's point of view.

LIFE PRINCIPLE: Only if the Holy Spirit is truly working in our hearts will we be able to have the compassion of God.

It is difficult to have compassion for others if we have been hurt or treated improperly by them. Describe an incident in your life that is a problem to you. How can the Holy Spirit help you to see the problem from God's point of view? How does God want to help you with your attitude?

_____

_____

_____

_____

_____

_____

_____

What does God's attitude toward the people of Nineveh show you about His attitude toward your sin? What does He want you to do about your sin? _____

_____

_____

34 THE MINOR PROPHETS

Previously we have studied what are known as the Major Prophets—Isaiah, Jeremiah, Ezekiel and Daniel. Now we begin a short study of the Minor Prophets. These are called "minor," not because they are unimportant, but because the length of their writings is so much shorter than those of the Major Prophets. Beginning with Hosea, the next twelve books are known as the Minor Prophets. List them below.

- _____
- _____
- _____
- _____
- _____
- _____
- _____
- _____
- _____
- _____
- _____
- _____

We are going to look at several of the shorter prophetic books. In each of them, God uses the prophets to warn Israel of what would happen if they failed to turn back to Him.

Hosea

Hosea 4 begins with the words, "Hear the word of the Lord." What is God's warning in verses 1-3? _____

_____

_____

_____

_____

_____

Joel

What is God's desire for the people in Joel 2:12-13? _____

_____

_____

_____

Obadiah

Obadiah has only one chapter and is the shortest book in the Old Testament. Turn to it and look at verses 3-4. These verses explain the problem the prophets had in trying to bring Israel back to God. Explain the following two statements to understand what was wrong.

► "The pride of your heart has deceived you." _____

_____

_____

► "Though you soar like the eagle...I will bring you down, declares the Lord." _____

_____

_____

_____

Now, in one word, explain what the key problem was. _____

Many New Testament Bible teachings are also found in the Old Testament. One example is found in Obadiah. In the New Testament, Galatians 6:7 says, "A man reaps what he sows." Read Obadiah 15 and copy the part that means the same thing as Galatians 6:7. _____

_____

_____

_____

_____

Malachi

We just saw how both the Old and New Testaments teach the same basic principles.

Another important Bible principle is found in Malachi 3:8-10. Compare these verses with Luke 6:38 and 2 Corinthians 9:6-8. Explain this principle of God. _____

_____

_____

_____

_____

_____

_____

Amos

Throughout the books of the prophets are the warnings of God against a disobedient and rebellious people. But God also reminds His people of those things He has promised them. We will look at two passages that show God's reminder of His promises.

The first is found in Amos 9:14-15. Though His people have rebelled against Him and have had to endure affliction for their lack of faith, still God makes a special promise to Israel. What is it? _____

_____

_____

_____

_____

_____

Habakkuk

Another promise of God is given in Habakkuk 3:18-19. The promise is evident as Habakkuk prays. What is it? _____

_____

_____

Conquering The Enemy

There are many lessons we can learn by studying the prophets of the Old Testament. First, we realize that *God will not overlook sin and rebellion against His Word*. He will, however, warn us when we begin to go the wrong way. He is looking for our repentance. He wants us to turn back to Him.

Secondly, *God will discipline His children for disobedience*. The warnings will come; God is very patient and merciful and does not wish to discipline—but willful disobedience will eventually be punished.

Finally, *God's promises are from everlasting to everlasting*. We can trust Him in all things. His warnings will come true, but the promises of His blessings are also secure.

Think of a situation in your own life in which you have seen these truths occur. Describe what happened using the following outline.

* * * * * *

■ Sin and a warning to repent: _____

_____

_____

■ Discipline for unrepented sin and rebellion: _____

_____

_____

■ A promise or blessing received: _____

_____

_____

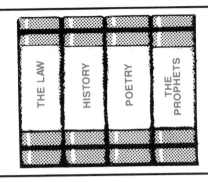

35
REVIEW

Multiple Choice

See how well you remember some of the facts we have studied this year. Choose the *best* answer to complete each of the following statements.

_____ 1. The book of beginnings is (a) Genesis (b) Psalms (c) Ecclesiastes.

_____ 2. The word that means "recovered or bought back from sin" is (a) salvation (b) redemption (c) justification.

_____ 3. Abraham's wife's name was (a) Leah (b) Rebekah (c) Sarah.

_____ 4. The son of Isaac who was a hunter was (a) Jacob (b) Esau (c) Benjamin.

_____ 5. Jacob's favorite son was (a) Joseph (b) Judah (c) Reuben.

_____ 6. Egypt is a picture of (a) righteousness (b) the world (c) God's faithfulness.

_____ 7. Moses' life can be divided into three periods of (a) 20 (b) 30 (c) 40 years each.

_____ 8. God sent (a) 7 (b) 10 (c) 15 plagues upon Egypt.

_____ 9. Moses received the Ten Commandments from the Lord on Mount (a) Ebal (b) Olivet (c) Sinai.

_____ 10. The Jewish tribe of priests was the tribe of (a) Gad (b) Levi (c) Reuben.

_____ 11. When the Israelites in the desert complained about being hungry, God sent (a) quail (b) turkeys (c) chickens for them to eat.

_____ 12. God's judgment on the unbelief of the Israelites in the wilderness was (a) they would no longer receive manna from heaven (b) all the spies who brought back a bad report were to be killed (c) all who were twenty years old or older would not be allowed to enter the Promised Land.

_____ 13. According to Deuteronomy 26:19, one of God's purposes for the people of Israel was that (a) they be different from everyone else (b) they be a holy people (c) they help advance civilization.

_____ 14. The Israelites gained their first victory in Canaan over the city of (a) Ai (b) Jericho (c) Hebron.

_____ 15. The judge whose army of 300 men defeated the Midianites was (a) Jephthah (b) Samson (c) Gideon.

_____ 16. When Ruth and her mother-in-law returned to Canaan, they settled in the town of (a) Jerusalem (b) Bethlehem (c) Nazareth.

_____ 17. The pattern of sin, servitude, repentance and deliverance summarizes the Book of (a) Exodus (b) Joshua (c) Judges.

_____ 18. The last judge of Israel was (a) Samson (b) Samuel (c) Saul.

_____ 19. The first king of Israel was (a) Samuel (b) Saul (c) Solomon.

_____ 20. A close friendship developed between David and Saul's son named (a) Jonathan (b) Samuel (c) Eli.

_____ 21. David showed the character trait of (a) modesty (b) loyalty (c) courage by refusing to harm King Saul.

_____ 22. The correct order of Israel's first three kings was (a) Saul, David, Solomon (b) David, Solomon, Saul (c) David, Saul, Solomon.

_____ 23. The highlight of Solomon's reign was (a) his wise answer to the two women who claimed to be the mother of the same baby (b) the building of the temple (c) the visit of the Queen of Sheba.

_____ 24. After Solomon's reign the nation of Israel was divided into two kingdoms called (a) Israel and Judah (b) Judah and Moab (c) Judea and Samaria.

_____ 25. The ministry of the prophet Elijah was continued by the prophet (a) Isaiah (b) Jeremiah (c) Elisha.

_____ 26. The Persian king who allowed many Jews to return to Israel was (a) Cyrus (b) Nebuchadnezzar (c) Nehemiah.

_____ 27. The man who was leader and teacher of the Jews who had returned to Jerusalem was (a) Ezra (b) Nehemiah (c) Artaxerxes.

_____ 28. The goal Nehemiah set for him and his people was to (a) reestablish the nation of Israel (b) rebuild the temple (c) rebuild the walls of Jerusalem.

_____ 29. The Jewish girl who became Queen of Persia was (a) Esther (b) Ruth (c) Elizabeth.

_____ 30. God allowed Satan to kill the animals, servants and children of a man named (a) David (b) Job (c) Eliphaz.

_____ 31. Most of the psalms were written by (a) Solomon (b) Moses (c) David.

_____ 32. The word that begins the Psalms is (a) "praise" (b) "sing" (c) "blessed."

_____ 33. Most of the Proverbs were written by (a) David (b) Solomon (c) Asaph.

_____ 34. One phrase that is used throughout the Book of Ecclesiastes is (a) "everything is meaningless" (b) "the fear of the Lord" (c) "listen to my sayings."

_____ 35. The prophet who saw a vision of God seated on a throne with angels surrounding Him was (a) Jeremiah (b) Isaiah (c) Daniel.

_____ 36. The prophet who saw a vision of a city with the name "The Lord is there" was (a) Ezekiel (b) Daniel (c) Isaiah.

_____ 37. The first conflict Daniel faced in Babylon involved the king's (a) diet (b) dream (c) image.

_____ 38. The Babylonian king who saw a hand writing on a wall during one of his banquets was (a) Nebuchadnezzar (b) Belshazzar (c) Darius.

_____ 39. The prophet who tried to run away from God by boarding a ship was (a) Elijah (b) Jonah (c) Haggai.

_____ 40. There are (a) 12 (b) 8 (c) 4 Minor Prophets in the Old Testament.

Seek And Find

Read the verses listed below and then find the characters mentioned in these verses in the following puzzle and circle each name.

Genesis 9:1
Exodus 4:10
Judges 6:39
Ruth 1:16
1 Samuel 3:20

1 Samuel 17:45
1 Kings 2:12
Esther 2:7
Job 1:1
Jonah 3:4

```
G  I  D  E  O  N  Z  Q  R  E  H  T  S  E
H  J  A  K  L  R  O  B  E  G  E  E  A  E
B  A  O  R  N  U  T  O  N  U  S  O  M  C
O  L  E  N  E  T  R  J  T  O  I  V  U  D
J  E  S  B  A  H  U  O  M  T  A  S  E  R
O  C  H  J  O  H  D  A  V  I  D  H  L  I
S  O  L  O  M  O  N  N  D  J  O  N  A  L
```

Name The Book

Match the following items, telling which Old Testament book records the event or applies to the statement. (Note: Each answer is only used once.)

_____ 1. David kills Goliath	A. Genesis
_____ 2. Written by David, Asaph, Moses and others	B. Exodus
_____ 3. Twelve spies are sent into Canaan	C. Leviticus
_____ 4. "The word of the Lord came to me"	D. Numbers
_____ 5. Naomi returns to Canaan	E. Deuteronomy
_____ 6. "There is a time and a season for everything"	F. Joshua
_____ 7. A leader who taught those who had returned to Jerusalem	G. Judges
_____ 8. Persian leaders are devoured by lions	H. Ruth
_____ 9. The tabernacle is built	I. 1 or 2 Samuel
_____ 10. The first of the Minor Prophets	J. 1 or 2 Kings
_____ 11. Immanuel would be born of a virgin	K. Ezra
_____ 12. The Israelites enter the Promised Land	L. Nehemiah
_____ 13. A prophet is unhappy when a city repents	M. Esther
_____ 14. Solomon asks God for wisdom	N. Job
_____ 15. Helps us grow in wisdom and understanding	O. Psalms
_____ 16. Joseph is sold as a slave	P. Proverbs
_____ 17. The last of the Minor Prophets	Q. Ecclesiastes
_____ 18. Artaxerxes' cupbearer makes a request	R. Isaiah
_____ 19. The story of Gideon	S. Jeremiah
_____ 20. Shows why God allows trials	T. Ezekiel
_____ 21. The shortest book of the Old Testament	U. Daniel
_____ 22. The main theme is "holiness"	V. Hosea
_____ 23. The captivity will end in seventy years	W. Obadiah
_____ 24. Haman is hanged instead of Mordecai	X. Jonah
_____ 25. Moses' last sermon	Y. Malachi

Who Am I?

Match the following descriptions with the correct corresponding Old Testament character.

_____ 1. I ministered to Eli at Shiloh.

_____ 2. I told Naaman to wash seven times in the Jordan River.

_____ 3. I was one of Joseph's brothers.

_____ 4. I went to Mount Nebo to die.

_____ 5. I was Isaac's wife.

_____ 6. I was thrown into a blazing furnace.

_____ 7. I complained and became a leper.

_____ 8. I was able to interpret dreams.

_____ 9. I was Jacob's deceptive uncle.

_____ 10. I was the father of Israel's second king.

_____ 11. I stole some gold from Jericho.

_____ 12. I sinned in the Garden of Eden.

_____ 13. I was called "the greatest man among all the people of the East."

_____ 14. I lied to Moses.

_____ 15. I went before the king of Persia and asked him not to kill the Jews.

_____ 16. I said the Israelites should take possession of the land of Canaan.

_____ 17. I told Ahab there would be no rain for three years.

_____ 18. I was the oldest man who ever lived.

_____ 19. I was a shepherd boy before I became king.

_____ 20. I was Jacob's second wife.

A. Job
B. Methuselah
C. Daniel
D. Elisha
E. Rachel
F. Achan
G. Zebulun
H. Adam
I. Elijah
J. Laban
K. Moses
L. David
M. Pharaoh
N. Jesse
O. Rebekah
P. Miriam
Q. Samuel
R. Caleb
S. Esther
T. Abednego

MUSIC CURRICULUM

September Hymn

HIS NAME IS WONDERFUL

His name is Wonderful, His name is Wonderful,
His name is Wonderful, Jesus, my Lord;
He is the mighty King, Master of ev'rything,
His name is Wonderful, Jesus, my Lord.
He's the great Shepherd, the Rock of all ages,
Almighty God is He;
Bow down before Him, love and adore Him,
His name is Wonderful, Jesus my Lord.

September Choruses

TELL ME THE STORIES OF JESUS

Tell me the stories of Jesus, I love to hear;
Things I would ask Him to tell me if He
were here;
Scenes by the wayside, tales of the sea,
Stories of Jesus, tell them to me.

First let me hear how the children stood
round His knee;
And I shall fancy His blessing resting on
me;
Words full of kindness, deeds full of grace
All in the love-light of Jesus' face.

Into the city I'd follow, the children's
band,
Waving a branch of the palm tree high in
my hand;
One of His heralds, yes, I would sing
Loudest hosannas! Jesus is King.

Tell me in accents of wonder, how rolled
the sea,
Tossing the boat in a tempest on Galilee!
And how the Master, ready and kind,
Chided the billows, and hushed the wind.

WHISPER A PRAYER

Whisper a prayer in the morning,
Whisper a prayer at noon,
Whisper a prayer in the evening
To keep your heart in tune.

God answers prayer in the morning,
God answers prayer at noon,
God answers prayer in the evening,
So keep your heart in tune.

Jesus may come in the morning,
Jesus may come at noon,
Jesus may come in the evening,
So keep your heart in tune.

PRAISE YE THE LORD

Praise ye the Lord! Praise ye the Lord!
O it is good to praise the Lord!

October Hymn

TRUST AND OBEY

When we walk with the Lord in the light of His Word,
What a glory He sheds on our way!
While we do His good will, He abides with us still
And with all who will trust and obey.

Not a shadow can rise, not a cloud in the skies,
But His smile quickly drives it away;
Not a doubt nor a fear, not a sigh nor a tear
Can abide while we trust and obey.

But we never can prove the delights of His love
Until all on the altar we lay;
For the favor He shows and the joy He bestows
Are for them who will trust and obey.

Then in fellowship sweet we will sit at His feet,
Or we'll walk by His side in the way;
What He says we will do, where He sends we will go—
Never fear, only trust and obey.

Refrain

Trust and obey, for there's no other way
To be happy in Jesus, but to trust and obey.

October Choruses

GET SMART

There's a broad way; there's a bright way,
There's a way that seems the right way;
But it's the wrong way, for it leads you
   far from God.

Travel God's way; it's the best way.
It's the only tried and true way,
And it will lead to life eternal some glad
   day.

Get smart! Take heart! Trust God! and
   start!
Travel God's way; it's the best way.
It's the only tried and true way,
And it will lead to life eternal some glad
   day.

THE BIBLE SAYS IT

The Bible says it, I believe it, I am saved
   by grace:
The Bible says it, I believe it, I am saved
   by grace:
Not by works which I have done, but
   thru faith in God's own Son:
The Bible says it, I believe it, I am saved
   by grace!

(Continued on next page)

October Chorus

HIS BANNER OVER ME IS LOVE

Jesus is the Rock of my salvation, His banner over me is love.
Jesus is the Rock of my salvation, His banner over me is love.
Jesus is the Rock of my salvation, His banner over me is love.
His banner over me is love!

November Hymn

BATTLE HYMN OF THE REPUBLIC

Mine eyes have seen the glory of the coming of the Lord;
He is trampling out the vintage where the grapes of wrath are stored;
He hath loosed the fateful lightning of His terrible swift sword:
His truth is marching on.

I have seen Him in the watchfires of a hundred circling camps;
They have builded Him an altar in the evening dews and damps;
I can read His righteous sentence by the dim and flaring lamps:
His day is marching on.

I have read a fiery gospel writ in burnished rows of steel:
"As ye deal with My contemners, so with you My grace shall deal;
Let the Hero, born of woman, crush the serpent with His heel,
Since God is marching on."

He has sounded forth the trumpet that shall never call retreat;
He is sifting out the hearts of men before His judgment seat;
O be swift, my soul, to answer Him! Be jubilant, my feet!
Our God is marching on.

In the beauty of the lilies Christ was born across the sea,
With a glory in His bosom that transfigures you and me:
As He died to make men holy, let us die to make men free,
While God is marching on.

Refrain

Glory! Glory! Hallelujah! Glory! Glory! Hallelujah!
Glory! Glory! Hallelujah! His truth is marching on. Amen.

November Chorus

I'M AN HEIR OF GOD

I'm an heir of God, and a joint heir with Jesus,
And the future is bright for me;
I'm an heir of God, and a joint heir with Jesus,
Oh, the wonder such a thing could be, Hallelujah!
For with Jesus, divine, all His shall be mine,
And I'm an heir, and a joint heir with Him.

(Continued on next page)

November Choruses

HOLY, HOLY, HOLY

Holy, holy, holy, Lord God Almighty!
Early in the morning our song shall rise
   to Thee;
Holy, holy, holy, merciful and mighty!
God in Three Persons, blessed Trinity!

Holy, holy, holy, tho' the darkness hide
   Thee,
Tho' the eye of sinful man Thy glory may
   not see,
Only Thou art holy; there is none beside
   Thee
Perfect in pow'r, in love, and purity.

Holy, holy, holy, Lord God Almighty!
All Thy works shall praise Thy name, in
   earth, and sky and sea;
Holy, holy, holy, merciful and mighty!
God in three Persons, blessed Trinity!

JESUS NEVER FAILS

Earthly friends may prove untrue,
Doubts and fears assail;
One still loves and cares for you,
One who will not fail.

Tho' the sky be dark and drear,
Fierce and strong the gale,
Just remember He is near
And He will not fail.

In life's dark and bitter hour
Love will still prevail;
Trust His everlasting pow'r—
Jesus will not fail.

Chorus

Jesus never fails, Jesus never fails;
Heav'n and earth may pass away,
But Jesus never fails.

December Hymn

SILENT NIGHT! HOLY NIGHT!

Silent night! Holy night!
All is calm, all is bright
Round yon virgin mother and Child
Holy Infant, so tender and mild—
Sleep in heavenly peace,
Sleep in heavenly peace.

Silent night! Holy night!
Shepherds quake at the sight;
Glories stream from heaven afar,
Heav'nly hosts sing alleluia!
Christ the Savior is born!
Christ the Savior is born!

Silent night! Holy night!
Son of God, love's pure light
Radiant beams from Thy holy face
With the dawn of redeeming grace—
Jesus, Lord, at Thy birth,
Jesus, Lord, at Thy birth.

January Hymn

I GAVE MY LIFE FOR THEE

I gave My life for thee, My precious blood I shed,
That thou might'st ransomed be, and quickened from the dead;
I gave, I gave My life for thee—What hast thou giv'n for Me?
I gave, I gave My life for thee—What hast thou giv'n for Me?

My Father's house of light, My glory circled throne,
I left, for earthly night, for wand'rings sad and lone;
I left, I left it all for thee—Hast thou left aught for Me?
I left, I left it all for thee—Hast thou left aught for Me?

I suffered much for thee, more than thy tongue can tell,
Of bitt'rest agony, to rescue thee from hell;
I've borne, I've borne it all for thee—What hast thou borne for Me?
I've borne, I've borne it all for thee—What hast thou borne for Me?

And I have brought to thee, down from My home above,
Salvation full and free, My pardon and My love;
I bring, I bring rich gifts to thee—What hast thou brought to Me?
I bring, I bring rich gifts to thee—What hast thou brought to Me?

January Chorus

THE LIGHT OF THE WORLD IS JESUS

The whole world was lost in the darkness of sin,
The light of the world is Jesus;
Like sunshine at noonday His glory shone in,
The light of the world is Jesus.

No darkness have we who in Jesus abide,
The light of the world is Jesus;
We walk in the Light when we follow our Guide,
The light of the world is Jesus.

No need of the sunlight in heaven we're told,
The light of the world is Jesus;
The Lamb is the Light in the City of Gold,
The light of the world is Jesus.

Chorus

Come to the Light, 'tis shining for thee;
Sweetly the Light has dawned upon me;
Once I was blind, but now I can see;
The light of the world is Jesus.

(Continued on next page)

GOD IS SO GOOD

God made so many lovely things,
And keeps them in His care,
Yet nothing is too big or small,
His tender love to share.

The sun drives all the clouds away,
The moon reflects its light;
The stars their silver torches wave;
God made the day and night.

God made the merry birds that sing,
The earth and sky and sea;
Tho' up in heav'n, He loves to bless
A little child like me.

Chorus

God is so good, so very good,
Our Father up above;
God is so good, so very good,
We'll give Him hearts of love.

WHEN YOUR FEARS GROW MOUNTAIN HIGH

When your fears grow mountain high,
And would block your pathway,
Wait, Oh, wait upon the Lord,
Believing while you pray.
Then your eagle wings will grow;
Up, up, up, up, up, you'll go!
Over! Hallelujah, over!
With the mountains far below!

February Hymn

IT TOOK A MIRACLE

My Father is omnipotent, and that you can't deny;
A God of might and miracles—'tis written in the sky.

Tho' here His glory has been shown, we still can't fully see
The wonders of His might, His throne—'twill take eternity.

The Bible tells us of His pow'r and wisdom all way thru,
And ev'ry little bird and flow'r are testimonies too.

Chorus

It took a miracle to put the stars in place,
It took a miracle to hang the world in space;
But when He saved my soul, cleansed and made me whole,
It took a miracle of love and grace.

February Choruses

EVERY DAY WITH JESUS

Ev'ry day with Jesus is sweeter than the
day before,
Ev'ry day with Jesus I love Him more
and more;
Jesus saves and keeps me, and He's the
One I'm waiting for;
Ev'ry day with Jesus is sweeter than the
day before.

WONDERFUL JESUS

Wonderful, wonderful Jesus!
Who can compare with Thee!
Wonderful, wonderful Jesus!
Fairer than all art Thou to me.
Wonderful, wonderful Jesus!
Oh, how my soul loves Thee!
Fairer than all the fairest,
Jesus, art Thou to me!

WIDE, WIDE AS THE OCEAN

Wide, wide as the ocean, high as the heavens above;
Deep, deep as the deepest sea is my Savior's love;
I, though so unworthy, still I'm a child of His care;
For His Word teaches me that His love reaches me ev'rywhere.

March Hymn

HE LIVES

I serve a risen Savior, He's in the world today;
I know that He is living, whatever men may say;
I see His hand of mercy, I hear His voice of cheer,
And just the time I need Him He's always near.

In all the world around me I see His loving care,
And tho' my heart grows weary I never will despair;
I know that He is leading, thro' all the stormy blast,
The day of His appearing will come at last.

Rejoice, rejoice, O Christian, lift up your voice and sing
Eternal hallelujahs to Jesus Christ the King!
The Hope of all who seek Him, the Help of all who find,
None other is so loving, so good and kind.

Refrain

He lives, He lives, Christ Jesus lives today!
He walks with me and talks with me along life's narrow way.
He lives, He lives, salvation to impart!
You ask me how I know He lives? He lives within my heart.

March Choruses

ROAR WENT THE LIONS

Roar! Roar! Roar! went the lions.
Down on his knees Daniel fell.
He knew the God who made the lions
Could shut their mouths as well;
And God heard him; oh yes, He heard
    him;
And He shut the lions' mouths up tight!
    tight! tight!
I'll be like Daniel bold,
Who lived in days of old.
I'll trust the Lord, let come what may;
I'll serve Him ev'ry day.

WHEN HE COMETH

When He cometh, when He cometh
To make up His jewels,
All His jewels, precious jewels,
His loved and His own.

He will gather, He will gather
The gems for His kingdom,
All the pure ones, all the bright ones,
His loved and His own.

Little children, little children
Who love their Redeemer,
Are the jewels, precious jewels
His loved and His own.

Chorus

Like the stars of the morning
His bright crown adorning,
They shall shine in their beauty,
Bright gems for His crown.

(Continued on next page)

March Chorus

ISN'T IT GRAND TO BE A CHRISTIAN

Isn't it grand to be a Christian, isn't it grand!
Isn't it grand to be a Christian, isn't it grand!
Isn't it grand to be a Christian,
Monday, Tuesday, Wednesday, Thursday, Friday, Saturday
And all day Sunday, isn't it grand!

Isn't it grand to work for Jesus, isn't it grand!
Isn't it grand to work for Jesus, isn't it grand!
Isn't it grand to work for Jesus,
Monday, Tuesday, Wednesday, Thursday, Friday, Saturday
And all day Sunday, isn't it grand!

Isn't it grand to look for Jesus, isn't it grand!
Isn't it grand to look for Jesus, isn't it grand!
Isn't it grand to look for Jesus,
Monday, Tuesday, Wednesday, Thursday, Friday, Saturday
And all day Sunday, isn't it grand!

April Hymn

IT IS WELL WITH MY SOUL

When peace, like a river, attendeth my way,
When sorrows like sea billows roll—
Whatever my lot, Thou hast taught me to say,
It is well, it is well with my soul.

Tho' Satan should buffet, tho' trials should come,
Let this blest assurance control,
That Christ hath regarded my helpless estate
And hath shed His own blood for my soul.

My sin—O the bliss of this glorious tho't—
My sin, not in part, but the whole,
Is nailed to the cross, and I bear it no more:
Praise the Lord, praise the Lord, O my soul!

And, Lord, haste the day when my faith shall be sight,
The clouds be rolled back as a scroll:
The trump shall resound and the Lord shall descend,
"Even so"—it is well with my soul.

Chorus

It is well with my soul,
It is well, it is well with my soul.

April Chorus

I BELIEVE

I believe in God the Father, who made us ev'ry one,
Who made the earth and heaven, the moon and stars and sun;
All that He gives each day, to us by Him is giv'n;
We call Him when we pray, "Our Father God in heav'n."

I believe in Jesus, Savior, the Father's only Son,
Who came to us from heaven, and loved us ev'ry one;
Upon the cross of Calv'ry He died to set us free;
And if we but receive Him, His children we will be.

I believe the Holy Spirit dwells in my heart today,
And that He leads and guides me along my pilgrim way.
The Father, Son and Spirit are the great One in Three;
We worship and adore them, the blessed Trinity.

(Continued on next page)

THAT'S WHY I LOVE HIM

Jesus has promised my Shepherd to be, that's why I love Him so;
And to the children He said, "Come to Me," that's why I love Him so.

He the weak lambs to His bosom will take, that's why I love Him so;
Never will He for a moment forsake, that's why I love Him so.

He has in heaven prepared me a place, that's why I love Him so;
Where I may dwell, by His wonderful grace, that's why I love Him so.

Chorus

That's why I love Him, that's why I love Him,
Because He first loved me;
When I'm tempted and tried, He is close by my side,
That's why I love Him so.

FOR GOD SO LOVED THE WORLD

For God so loved the world He gave His only Son
To die on Calvary's tree, from sin to set me free;
Some day He's coming back, what glory that will be!
Wonderful His love to me.

May Hymn

I SURRENDER ALL

All to Jesus I surrender, all to Him I freely give;
I will ever love and trust Him, in His presence daily live.

All to Jesus I surrender, humbly at His feet I bow;
Worldly pleasures all forsaken, take me, Jesus, take me now.

All to Jesus I surrender, make me, Savior, wholly Thine;
Let me feel the Holy Spirit—truly know that Thou art mine.

All to Jesus I surrender, Lord, I give myself to Thee;
Fill me with Thy love and power, let Thy blessings fall on me.

Chorus

I surrender all, I surrender all,
All to Thee, my blessed Savior, I surrender all.

May Chorus

JESUS LOVES EVEN ME

I am so glad that our Father in heav'n
Tells of His love in the book He has giv'n;
Wonderful things in the Bible I see;
This is the dearest, that Jesus loves me.

Tho' I forget Him and wander away,
Still He doth love me wherever I stray;
Back to His dear loving arms would I flee,
When I remember that Jesus loves me.

Oh, if there's only one song I can sing,
When in His beauty I see the great King,
This shall my song in eternity be,
"Oh, what a wonder that Jesus loves me."

Chorus

I am so glad that Jesus loves me,
Jesus loves me, Jesus loves me,
I am so glad that Jesus loves me,
Jesus loves even me.

(Continued on next page)

JESUS LOVES ME

Jesus loves me! This I know, for the Bible tells me so;
Little ones to Him belong, they are weak but He is strong.

Jesus loves me! He who died heaven's gate to open wide;
He will wash away my sin, let His little child come in.

Jesus loves me! He will stay close beside me all the way;
He's prepared a home for me, and some day His face I'll see.

Chorus

Yes, Jesus loves me! Yes, Jesus loves me!
Yes, Jesus loves me! The Bible tells me so.

HE'S THE ONE I LOVE

He's the One I love, He's the One I love,
Fairer is He than the lily to me, He's the One I love.